for the love of God

Thirtysix.org

For the Love of God

Expanding the Capacity for the Greatest Pleasure of All

ISBN 9798666754627

Published by:
Thirtysix.org
22 Yitzchak Road
Telzstone, Kiryat Yearim
Israel   9083800

"And you shall love the Lord your **God** with all your heart(s)."

	Introduction	7
1	Love God	13
2	Soul Love, Only Love	25
3	Entitlement	33
4	Love the Goal	41
5	Wall in the Way	51
6	Love of a Parent	63
7	Purim Love	69
8	Chanukah Love	85
9	Love, By Definition	101
10	Prayer of Love	113
11	Land of Love	123
	Other Books	135

RECENTLY A RELATIVE told me about a story I had heard before, though I could not recall where. It is about a man in the camps who had been taken out by a Nazi to be hanged. He was asked if there were anything he wanted before he was killed. He requested his tefillin, which he was given.

As he put on his tefillin, he noticed that Jews who had been collected to watch the killing were crying, and he told them. "Don't be sad. I am happy to be doing this," as he sanctified the Name of God one last time.

When the German soldier saw that the Jew was enjoying himself, he pulled him down from the platform and gave him a bunch of rocks to hold. He said, "If you drop any of these rocks, I will shoot you," and then proceeded to beat the Jew 29 times. By some miracle, the Jew didn't drop a single rock and, what is even more miraculous, he survived the war.

As I listened to the story, a little voice inside me said, "Hashem! This man was risking his last moments of life to sanctify Your Name, and he even derived enjoyment from the sacrifice. He CLEARLY loved YOU, and this is how YOU responded? By having the enemy take away his tefillin and mercilessly beat him?"

True, his life was saved, but was there no other more peaceful way to do that? Couldn't there have been a fire, or an air raid…or something else to interrupt the Nazi brutality? Why did this prisoner have to go through what he did? We saw his love. Where was God's?

The truth is that it did not start or end there. We can go back to Rebi Akiva, who suffered humiliation when he became a ba'al teshuvah at the age of 40 and devoted the rest of his life to Torah. The angels themselves questioned the manner of his death,[1] Rebi Akiva should have passed from this world peacefully, rather than being tortured by the vicious Romans until his dying moment!

Where was God's love then?

My experience, on the other hand, has been different. I think I have always loved God, but even more

---

[1] Brochos 61b.

so as I get older. And I love to do things to show that I love Him. But I have to admit, when something backfires or doesn't bring the kind of positive results I expected, I am disappointed, confused, even frustrated. To use the language of the Talmud, I sort of kick the succah on the way out.[2] Love is a two-way street, right?

Wrong, at least not when it comes to God. True, the Mishnah does advocate unconditional love between people,[3] but not to the point that you withstand abuse. When humans don't reciprocate love, it can be an indication of something wrong. You may love someone with no expectations, but you certainly shouldn't turn a blind eye to an abusive and unappreciative partner, who certainly means you harm even if he can't help himself.

When it comes to God, however, we say, "All that God does He does for the good."[4]

But what if it was for the bad?

That's what it says: All that GOD does, He does for the GOOD. It means that whatever may seem like the worst thing possible to us is still, ultimately and by definition, for the good. That is why He is called "God," like the word "good," to remind us that God,

---

2 Avodah Zarah 3b.

3 Pirkei Avos 5:19.

4 Brochos 61b.

by His very nature, does only good.

This would not have been so hard to see had the first man not messed things up by eating from the Aitz HaDa'as Tov v'Ra, the Tree of Knowledge of Good and Evil. Man at the beginning was straightforward, and therefore God could be straightforward with him. Good was good and bad was bad, and never the twain could meet.

When Adam sinned, however, and ate from the forbidden fruit, he changed EVERYTHING. He especially changed the way God worked with us because kabbalistically Adam caused good and evil to mix, with the result that good was in evil and vice-versa.[5] This made history and Hashgochah Pratis–Divine Providence murky.

Accepting Torah at Mt. Sinai 2,448 years later, we had the opportunity to reverse the sin of Adam HaRishon and set things right once again. But that too was short-lived, when the Erev Rav—the Mixed Multitude whose very name implies the mixture of good and evil—built the golden calf.[6] That undid just about all the rectification of Kabbalas HaTorah, making history and Divine Providence murky once again.

Accepting on faith that God only does good is the way we survive the deceptions of history. It means

---

[5] Drushei Olam HaTohu, Chelek 2, Drush 4, Anaf 4.
[6] Shemos 32:1.

a ONE-WAY outpouring of love for God, from us to Him. He does not need to perform acts that WE can perceive as GOOD, so they can therefore be interpreted by us as acts of love. He loves us. He always has. He always will. He may hate evil, but He loves us, and that is the greatest given of life there is.

The variable in our relationship with God is not HIS love, but OUR love. How far are we prepared to go to love Him? How unconditional can we make our love of God? How strong does our love need to be so that it won't bend under the pressure of what seems to us to be divine abandonment? These are the only questions that should concern us.

Loving God does not entitle us to anything, at least not in this world. It will entitle us to EVERYTHING in the NEXT WORLD. In this world it is a tremendous merit to be able to love God, and to find ways to express that love. Fortunate and blessed is the one who truly feels love of God in his heart. Happy will be the one who can experience that without looking for signs of God's love in return.

Make no mistake about it. If you truly love God, then God will truly love you—and the truth is that He will love you even if you don't return the love. And also make no mistake about the fact that He loves to show you His love in this world too, when the situation allows. But the one mistake you should NEVER EVER make is that if YOUR love of God does not result in what you think should be an act of HIS love, that it means HIS love isn't there.

It IS there, more than we can ever know, for now at least. Later, when history comes to a close and the yetzer hara is no more, with all evil gone from the world, we'll see the truth. And we'll be overwhelmed by just how much God has ALWAYS loved us.

ALWAYS.

THERE IS A mitzvah to love God, and we repeat it at least twice a day when saying the Shema: "You shall love the Lord your God…"[1] Given what God has done for us, and continues to do for us, it is obvious that we should love God.

The part that is not obvious is what happens if you don't. What do you do if you don't yet love God? It's not as if you can just turn love on or off on a dime. How can you command people to feel any emotion they do not already have?

The Rambam answers that question here:

What is the process for coming to love and fear God? When one contemplates His actions and

---

[1] Devarim 6:5.

His wondrous and great creations, and sees in them His wisdom, that it has no limit and no end, immediately he will love and praise Him, and desire tremendously to know His great Name. (Yad Chazakah, Yesodei HaTorah, 2:2)

In one paragraph the Rambam tells us what love is all about. Even more than the body is wired to fall in love with a person's appearance, the soul is wired to love that which is spiritually amazing. Since the soul depends on the body to see, hear, taste, smell, and feel the outside world, it has a difficult time from inside a body to sense God if the body is not tuned in as well.

Tune the body in, let the soul sense God's greatness, says the Rambam, and love of God will automatically flow. Like two soulmates destined for each other from before birth, they have no idea about one another until they finally meet. But once they do, it's as if they were never apart, and they remain together forever.

But it's more than that. Who creates such an awesome world with billions of stars and galaxies for a single planet inhabited by a lowly being called man? That question should appear even before we learn what Creation looks like on the spiritual side of reality. That is far more awesome than the physical one we are still trying to grasp!

Anyone who appreciates the opportunity of life can't help but see "God loves me" written all over the world. If a pampered person walks into someone else's simchah, is fed like a king, and then complains about what he didn't get, we'd be angry—perhaps even despise him. His sense of entitlement and therefore his sense of something lacking would not endear him to anyone.

Let's face it, we have been given this remarkably generous world as a gift that we did nothing to earn. Putting aside the suffering for now—because it too has to be addressed—the world is quite a paradise outside the real paradise. We can only pat ourself on the back for what we have done with it because God gave both us and the world the potential to accomplish what we have already achieved.

Any corruption of Creation is man's. We can blame God all we want for what goes wrong in the world, and we sometimes want to do that a lot, but it is really our own doing. God gave us a yetzer hara to challenge us to be good of our own volition, and instead we make it the head of our household and follow its commands into meaninglessness.

We've been warned about doing that, and told the consequences for such capitulation. Parashas Bechukosai and Parashas Ki Savo, among others, explicitly state what will happen to Jewish history when people put allegiance to their yetzer haras over their allegiance to God and Torah.

Life is a test, but it wasn't created to be. We were created to go to the World-to-Come and never be tested again. We were created to go there and enjoy eternal pleasure with never a negative or dull moment. It's just that to get there—for our own good and BECAUSE God loves us—we have to face challenges and tests in this world so we can get to and enjoy the next one.

We think it is unnecessary. God can do anything, so why didn't He just create us in the World-to-Come from the start. We could have skipped this world that can give rise to the kind of destruction described in Parashiyos Bechukosai and Ki Savo, and gone right to the next one where everything is paradise.

That's only because we look at life from our limited perspective, which is very influenced by our aversion to pain. We prefer life to be easy, and we like to make life easier for the people we care about. Somehow we know that our quality of life goes up in sync with our struggle to accomplish, but that voice often gets drowned out by the pampered part of us that demands more and more physical pleasure.

There is a story told, supposedly true, of someone who before death promised to be an advocate on behalf of the loved one who survived. As it happened, the niftar returned during a dream to the one still living and said that he could not work to change anything for the better. In heaven, he explained, everything on earth was good, and there was no reason to change it!

The point is that no matter how destructive history gets—and that can't possibly happen without God's direct involvement—it is never a contradiction of His love for man. No matter how fierce and strong God's wrath may wax, it is just a mask over His innate love for His creations.

It's a hard sell, especially to people who have felt the brunt of that wrath in very painful and permanent ways. But none of it would have been necessary had man not messed up in the first place. If life is complicated, it is because man complicated it. And even that is somehow ultimately for our own good.

This was the completion of Nachum Ish Gamzu's famous statement. His name was literally "Nachum, man of gam zu," because after anything bad he would say, "Gam zu l'tovah—this too is for the good!" So "gam zu" became his last name, and many stories about him make it clear why. This is one of them:

> Nachum of Gam Zu was blind in both eyes, both his arms had been amputated, both legs had been amputated, and his entire body was covered in boils. He lay in a dilapidated house, and the legs of his bed were placed in buckets of water so that ants should not climb on him…

His students said to him: "Rebi, since you are a completely righteous man, why has this happened to you?"

He answered them: "I brought it on myself. Once I was traveling along the road to my father-in-law's house, and I had a load [distributed among] three donkeys, one of food, one of drink, and one of delicacies. A poor person came and stood [before me] in the road and said: 'Rebi, sustain me.' I told him: 'Wait until I unload the donkey,' [but] I did not manage to unload the donkey before he died. [Distraught] I went and fell on his face and said: 'May my eyes, which had no compassion on your eyes, be blinded! May my hands, which had no compassion on your hands, be amputated! May my legs, which had no compassion on your legs, be amputated!' My mind did not rest until I said: 'May my whole body be covered in boils!'"

[His students] said to him: "[Even so,] woe to us that we have seen you like this!"

He told them: "Woe is me if you had not seen me in this [state]!" (Ta'anis 21a)

What Nachum Ish Gamzu meant was that his absolutely horrific situation was really the best one for him, given what happened to him. For his students it seemed to be a reason to mourn, but he was grateful to be in it because it meant that he would go to the next world already cleansed of his terrible sin!

His terrible sin? What terrible sin did Nachum do? What were the odds—or indications—that taking just a few minutes to unload his donkey to feed the poor man on the road would be a few minutes too many? The man standing there with a request made it appear as if just the opposite were the case.

True, when it comes to the mitzvah of tzedakah, we do not delay. That's one of the reasons we don't make a blessing before performing the mitzvah, so as to not delay it even for a quick blessing! But if you have to reach into your wallet to find the money to give, or even go to another part of your house to find it, it's all part of the mitzvah. Nachum surely knew all this and acted according to it.

What happened to Nachum was clearly Hash-gochah Pratis, arranged by God. Under normal cir-cumstances he would have been able to unload his donkey, help the poor person, and be on his way. And given his level of righteousness, as his students point-ed out, God would have known that Nachum was not even capable of being careless or insensitive, and yet…

Here's another example of such questionable Divine Providence:

When they took Rebi Akiva out to be executed,

it was the time for saying the Shema. They combed his flesh with iron combs while he accepted on himself the yoke of the kingdom of heaven. His students said to him, "Our teacher, even until this point?"

He answered them, "All my life I have been pained by the verse, 'with all of your soul' [Devarim 6:5], which means even if He takes your soul. I have asked myself, 'When will I be able to fulfill this?' Now that I have a chance to do so, I shouldn't fulfill it?"

His soul left him as he was extending the word "echad" [of the Shema]. (Brochos 61b)

It's a curious question that the students of Rebi Akiva asked him. "Until this point?" What? Stay loyal to God? Trust Him? Stand up for Torah and mitzvos against the Romans? As Rebi Akiva answered them, "If not now, when? My whole life has been for this moment, and I should squander it with bitterness and fear? No, thank you, not me!"

How could his students even ask such a question at such an important time? These weren't yeshivah ketanah students with much to learn. Each student was a Torah giant in his own right who would have died the same way if necessary. From people like this, the question should instead have been a statement.

And why WAS Rebi Akiva looking forward to

such an opportunity his entire life? He had already gone to the greatest of lengths because of his love of God. What was left to prove? He already loved God with all his heart and with all his possessions. That is already loving God with all your life!

But how do you know? How do people ever know if they really gave God everything out of love, before they actually do it? Perhaps there is still more? Unless of course there isn't—BECAUSE of that love. That is what Rebi Akiva's students marveled at while watching their beloved rebi make one last, supreme sacrifice to God with ALL HIS HEART.

It was not the only way to go at that time. Many others facing a similar existential moment went the other way. They didn't die peacefully and joyously, proclaiming God's unity. They frantically and desperately claimed just the opposite, if not in words then at least in deed. They're the ones who made it worthwhile for the executioners to act so inhumanely.

The truth is that although we admire the Rebi Akivas of history, we might relate more to the other group. How many people don't feel abandoned when they are made to suffer? How can they not feel rejected when they fail, while so many others succeed? How can they feel the love of God when their dreams end up being nightmares? How can they avoid turning against Him because they feel God has turned against them? People have given up on God for a lot less.

The difference between one type of person and another can be profoundly deep on the soul level. Or it can have to do with upbringing and the attitude toward life developed while growing up and forming beliefs. Or it can be due to a life-altering incident experienced later in life that left someone bitter.

You can call it the glass-half-full or glass-half-empty attitude toward God's love of man. The greatest gift a parent or teacher can give a child is a sense of God's love, how deep and how profound it is. This knowledge is probably the greatest asset a person can have, which is why it is barely taught, if at all. The Sitra Achra doesn't want to make it easier for us to connect and remain connected to God, especially as he tests our spiritual resolve.

Arming a child with love of God is like arming a soldier for war. The greater the soldier's protection, the safer he will be. The more powerful his weapons are, the greater his chance of vanquishing as opposed to being vanquished.

Love of God works similarly. If people know how to look at the world and see past all the negative things that distract from how amazing God's creation is, they are spiritually fortified against anything. People for whom God's love is a given have received the greatest tool possible for getting through life on the highest level possible, as did Rebi Akiva and all those who lived and died like him.

THAT is what he answered his students that day. They were amazed that his love of God went THAT far. He told them that it had to, given how much he believed God loved him. They were overtaken with grief at the loss of their rebi, especially in such a way. But that day they also learned—from one of the most credible teachers ever—just how deeply a person can know the love of God.

Soul Love, Only Love

LOVE IS A function of the soul. The yetzer hara and all those who work for it would be delighted to make you believe that love is a body thing. But anyone who understands love knows that it just can't be, because the body is missing the most important component that makes love possible.

The Torah spells it out at the beginning:

And Adam knew—yada his wife, Chava. (Bereishis 4:1)

The Torah is of course talking about physical intimacy. The question is whether the Torah is merely being polite by using the word "knew" or teaching us something about the true nature of love, as well as the basis for such intimacy.

This question does not exist in Kabbalah. In Kabbalah da'as–knowledge is a key concept and the basis for just about everything, especially love. It's not as simple as "to know someone is to love him," but this expression is on the right track.

Da'as, according to Kabbalah, is called koach hachibur—the power of unification. Love also unifies, which the Hebrew word hints at. In Hebrew love is ahavah, with a gematria of 13, the same as the word echad–one. The equation is simple: Da'as equals love.

To appreciate this it is important to better understand the role of emotions in life.

Reality is something we take for granted. It is real and we are part of it. But many people have questioned this. Depressed people complain about feeling detached from reality, as if they are living in a dream, a bad dream.

When something really exciting happens that evokes a tremendous emotional reaction from us, we often feel the most real. That feeling is so enlivening that people parachute from airplanes, take death-defying roller-coaster rides, and even pay money to be scared to death—among many other emotion-charging activities—just to feel more alive.

Try telling someone how much you love him or her without any emotion. How does it feel when someone tells you the same thing in the same way?

Why do we have a hard time believing it, even from people who give us things and take care of our needs? Why does it matter so much what's in a person's HEART? Isn't it enough just to be in a person's HEAD?

It matters because not only are emotions a bridge to reality, they're also our bridge to one another. Emotions are unnecessary for something bodiless because in that state only truth exists. Whatever exists conceptually is by definition truth. And the truth, which is called the "seal of God,"[1] binds EVERYTHING together as one.

That is koach hachibur of da'as. The more truthful the da'as is, the greater will be its power to unify.

After the sin of eating from the Aitz HaDa'as Tov v'Ra, the Tree of Knowledge of Good and Evil, bodies became more physical and therefore more intrusive.[2] Before entering the body, two souls could share an intimate moment through knowledge alone. Within the body there is so much background noise that souls don't even notice one another without a lot of work.

That is what Purim, a holiday of da'as, teaches. Wine, associated with da'as,[3] neutralizes the body so

---

[1] Yoma 69b.

[2] Hakdamos u'Sha'arim, Sha'ar 6, Ch. 10.

[3] Eiruvin 64a.

that souls can converse—both with God and with one another. That is why the holiday of Purim corresponds to a high level of the World-to-Come and the sefirah of Chochmah—Wisdom, which is the first level of da'as.[4]

Yom HaKippurim as well. It corresponds to the sefirah of Binah and the stage of the World-to-Come just prior to the one that corresponds to Purim. Therefore rabbis play on the word kippurim, reading it as k'Purim—like Purim, because we're supposed to achieve through fasting and prayer what we achieve through wine and joy on Purim: disembodiment and freedom of the soul.

Hence "Adam KNEW his wife, Chava." When they were first created, their bodies were more like souls than our bodies today.[5] They had yet to have yetzer haras, which makes bodies so intrusive. They could be intimate as souls more intensely than any bodies could be on their own. The pleasure their bodies felt was in fact the da'as of the soul coursing through their spinal cords.[6]

Then came the sin, followed by the transforma-

---

[4] The light of Keser, the highest sefirah, is being filtered through the sefiros of Chochmah and Binah to become the sefirah of Da'as (Klallei Haschalos HaChochmah).

[5] Hakdamos u'Sha'arim, Sha'ar 6, Ch. 10.

[6] Drushei Olam HaTohu, Drush Aitz HaDa'as, Siman 3.

tion. Adam's skin of light became a skin of flesh, also called "skin of the snake," because of the snake's role in the sin.[7] It was as if the soul were locked away in a soundproof, windowless chamber, its life force harnessed and its access to the world greatly limited. The world started belonging to the body—as people began following their yetzer haras—and this has continued ever since.

But the body is usually its own worst enemy. It wants pleasure but without the necessary work. It's willing to cheat to have that pleasure, even kill for it. And yet after thousands of years of trying to hone the art of soulless pleasure, it can't understand why it doesn't have it. Consequently it just keeps adding soulless pleasure to soulless pleasure in its never-ending search for what it always had right inside itself.

What we call love is really the language of the body, which is why it is only felt in the body. It's an emotional response to a spiritual reality. The body, being physical and highly vulnerable to pain, instinctually protects itself and is rarely convinced by what intellect has to say, even its own. It wants to FEEL the truth of an idea before it will lower its defenses and let the outside in, before it will unify with something beyond itself.

There's more. Kabbalah explains that this is a

---

[7] Drushei Olam HaTohu, Drush Aitz HaDa'as, Siman 4.

world of action, or more accurately, of actualization.[8] Both good and evil are only potentials until actualized by a person as either a good deed or a bad one. If an idea does not make it into action because of a person's lack of will, the intention will count for very little if anything at all.

Real love therefore is the actualization of da'as. It can't be anything else. If it isn't, then it isn't true love, only infatuation, the body's desire to have a love experience without the soul's involvement. But if the soul can't enjoy the relationship the body is having, then the experience is basically no different from that felt by gorging on food just to satisfy an unbridled, unhealthy, bodily passion.

This is why the Torah only permits certain kinds of relationships and does not allow physically intimacy without marital commitment. Everything we do down here is in order to strengthen our unification with God, the ULTIMATE pleasure in life and THE pleasure in the World-to-Come.[9] If a pleasure is not GODLY, then it is not REAL pleasure.

It is one thing to be drunk on love and quite another to be drunk on infatuation. A person who is drunk on alcohol thinks he is having real pleasure too, but it is artificial and short-lived. But someone who can

---

8 Drushei Olam HaTohu, Chelek 1, Drush 6, Siman 4, Os 3.

9 Chelek HaBiurim, Drushei Igulim v'Yoshar, Anaf 1, Os 1.

become drunk on life usually does so because he is involved in meaningful accomplishments, and they last forever.

Likewise, people who satisfy an infatuation feed the body and not the soul, creating nothing meaningful while cheapening the pleasure. It doesn't mean they will avoid the same mistakes next time, because some people never notice how much of life they have wasted until it begins to end. The world has been filled with such people for thousands of years.

However, people who pursue and achieve real love—which can only develop over time as one comes to know the soul of another—build something eternal. And not only is a real and lasting relationship created with another, since such a relationship is godly, it enhances one's relationship with God.

We live today in a very layered society. As if the body weren't enough of an interposition between souls to begin with, the situation has become worse by layers being added to layers. The emphasis on external and superficial values when people present themselves to the world has basically shut away the souls of people and cheapened the idea of love.

Just think of it. Desires to make tons of money resulted in industries and attitudes that reduced the average individual's capacity for true and lasting love. The love of many today, by virtue of its disassociation with the soul, is but a knockoff of the real thing, like cheap metal sprayed to look like gold. No wonder it peels off so easily.

So as people claim independence from God and the soul, the yetzer hara smiles at the success of its masterful deception of billions of people! Promising the fulfillment of their dreams of achieving the most prized emotion known to man, it keeps pulling a fast one, replacing true love with a much cheaper version, while making off with the profit.

Entitlement

WE HAVE ALL probably felt a sense of entitlement at some time or another, that feeling that we deserve something and that as far as we are concerned, it belongs to us. If we happen to get what we want, we feel justice has been served. If we don't, we feel as if we have been wronged by the entire universe.

It is obvious that such a feeling flies in the face of being happy with one's portion.[1] How can you possibly be happy with your portion if you think someone else has illicitly taken a part of it? You certainly can't experience the love of God if you're convinced that He didn't protect that love, and save you from loss and injustice.

The more entitled people feel, the more the feel-

---

[1] Pirkei Avos 4:1.

ing of injustice will be reinforced. People will constantly be upset over perceived losses and unfairness. Or they will just go and take what they believe is theirs, which will clearly not leave them on favorable terms with God or the people they are robbing.

Obviously people have to protect what they truly own. We're not obligated to take injustices lying down. There are laws in Choshen Mishpat[2] that specifically instruct people to protect what is legally theirs and how to go about doing it. Taking property for granted is also a grave mistake.

We're not talking about that now. We're talking about the things in life that WE believe should belong to us, but God disagrees. If He didn't disagree, we'd already have those things. Never confuse the means with the end. People and things may stand in the way of our success, but all of them work only for God in the end and, as mentioned previously, for OUR own good.

Where does this belief that one is inherently deserving of privileges or special treatment come from?

People who feel entitled have a higher sense of belief in their own importance than in the equality of all individuals or of society as a whole. Their focus is not on what is fair to everyone, but rather on what is

---

[2] The section of the Shulchan Aruch dealing with monetary deals and infractions.

not fair to them.

The operative term here is self-belief. What people think about themselves determines whether they will feel entitled in a given situation or not. Humble people do not feel entitled. Arrogant people do. The rest of us may lean to one side or the other, depending on what we think about ourself and the situation we are in at the time.

For example, people who consider themselves smart might be offended and feel left out if their opinion is not sought among people they deem to be equals or inferiors. But these same people will happily go unnoticed when they are among people they view as geniuses and superiors—unless their egos are so bloated that they foolishly consider themselves as equals.

This is every human's struggle. Too much belief in oneself leads to arrogance and results in situations that are often embarrassing, if not downright dangerous. Too little self-belief leads to insecurity and debilitation. A meaningful and productive life lies somewhere between the two extremes, and life is the process of finding that point, even creating it. Historically there have not been many people who successfully did that.

Everyone is entitled to self-belief; it says so right here:

God said, "Let us make man in our image, after our likeness…" (Bereishis 1:26)

Rashi explains that "our" really means "Mine," as in God's image and likeness. This means that EVERY human EVER created, no matter how handsome or how ugly, how talented or how inept, was made in the image of God. And although there has been a lot of discussion as to exactly what this means, one thing is for certain: every human being bears some aspect of divine perfection.

Once Rebi Elazar, son of Rebi Shimon, was coming from Migdal Gedor, from the house of his teacher. He rode along the riverside on his donkey and was feeling happy and elated because he had studied much Torah. He happened to meet a very ugly man who greeted him, "Peace be on you, my master!"

Rebi Elazar did not return the greeting but instead said to him, "How ugly this person is! Are all the people of your city as ugly as you?"

"I do not know," the man said. "But go to the craftsman who made me and tell him: 'How ugly is the vessel which you have made!'"

Realizing that he had been wrong, Rebi Elazar dismounted from his donkey, prostrated himself before the man, and said to him, "You are right.

Forgive me!" (Ta'anis 20a)

How easy it is to forget that every living creature, especially a person, is God's handiwork. Even as great a Torah scholar as Rebi Elazar ben Rebi Shimon did so and treated the man he encountered virtually as sub-human. But the man wisely rebuked him by mentioning his divine origin, and within seconds Rebi Elazar was humbled before him, begging to be forgiven.

There is a similar story that gets to the soul of the matter:

> The daughter of the emperor said to Rebi Yehoshua ben Chananya, "Too bad that glorious wisdom [like yours] is in [such] an ugly vessel!"
>
> So he asked her, "Does your father keep his wine in simple clay vessels?"
>
> She answered: "In what, then, should he keep it?"
>
> He said, "Important people like you should put it in gold and silver containers!"
>
> She went and told this to her father. He put the wine in vessels of gold and silver and it turned sour. [When his advisors] came and told the emperor [that the wine had turned sour], he asked [his daughter], "Who told you to do this?"
>
> She told him: "Rebi Yehoshua ben Chananya."
>
> [So the emperor] summoned him and asked:

"Why did you say this to her?"

[Rebi Yehoshua] told him: "As she spoke to me, so I spoke to her [to show her that fine material is best preserved in the least of vessels]."

[The emperor asked him:] "But aren't there handsome people who are learned?"

[Rebi Yehoshua replied:] "Had they been ugly, they would have been even more learned." (Ta'anis 7a)

Rebi Yehoshua and the emperor's daughter had been discussing wisdom, but it could have just as easily been a discussion about the soul. In fact they really are one and the same, wisdom and the soul, the former flowing from the latter. The soul tends to be better in a simpler vessel.

It is no coincidence that the more beautiful a generation becomes, the more people seem to feel entitled as well. No one is saying that anything is wrong with being attractive, wealthy, or careful to dress nicely. Judging by the natural beauty of the world, there is something godly about that too. We're just saying that those specific physical attributes often complicate matters when it comes to the ability of the soul to do what it was sent here to do: tikun–rectification.

That is why we are impressed when we meet someone who is both handsome, beautiful, or rich

AND also humble. We know that these are not likely combinations. People are drawn to success because they want it for themselves and tend to idolize those who appear to have achieved it, which makes it hard for the successful to keep their egos at bay.

In a society run by the yetzer hara, pursuing material success is the way to go. Emphasis on material success and pleasures makes it difficult for spiritual values to have much of a say. All attention is shifted toward society's idea of success, and society isn't even sure if the soul exists!

The problem is that physically we're not all equal. In fact there are HUGE discrepancies in physical attributes such as appearance and wealth. These differences make life very cliquey and jealousy incredibly likely. Equality is demanded where it cannot exist, resulting in a tremendous sense of entitlement with few ways of achieving it.

There can only be backlash in the end.

Because of their material shortcomings some people have either left the system or never had a chance to enter it. Leaving the system may not have been their original intention. Perhaps at first they were just envious of others who had credentials to rise to the top of society that they themselves lacked, so they decided instead to find another direction.

And while doing that, they tended to notice other traits and values that, lo and behold, were FAR more valuable. Values like humility, wisdom, kindness, modesty, etc. Perhaps they noticed it happening, perhaps they didn't, but in the process they tended to become really fine people with a great sense of appreciation and little sense of entitlement. These people built worlds—rather than destroy them—to get what they thought was coming to them.

And the really important thing is that during the process they could FEEL the love of God. They didn't have any resentment or misguided ambition to get in the way. We have only so much emotional energy, and when channeled in one direction, it cannot be channeled in another at the same time. People who do not feel entitled are less emotionally distracted, and that leaves them open to feel the love of God.

Love the Goal

YOU HAVE TO love the goal because the goal IS love. Wherever you go in the world, love is high priority. We start with our own parents, then move on to friends, and eventually to a spouse. People go "bad" because of insufficient or corrupted love. People who get the right kind of love at the right time tend to make the most of their lives.

One amazing thing about humans is how they can value something so much and yet take it so for granted, as if it were the most obvious given. Yet a single crisis can shatter the illusion and make people reevaluate what they previously didn't value enough. Around the world marriage therapists are kept busy with such people.

But as much as love is really for the loved one,

the reality is that we benefit greatly by giving it as well, maybe even more than those receiving it. Recipients only get to enjoy the love someone else gives them, whereas the ones doing the loving get to feel good both about the love they give and the love it evokes in response. So yes, love must be selflessly given for it to work. But no, that doesn't mean that we too don't benefit greatly from giving it, which is another wonderful thing about being human and about love.

Many people seem to look at love as a side show, like popcorn they eat while watching an exciting film. The main goal in life for many is personal success—for some material, for others spiritual, and for a very few both. The love they give and get is incidental on their way to this end.

They have it backwards. We actually live to love, or at least we should. There is a strong sense of lack in the world, and all the resentment that goes along with it, which people seem to think has to do with a shortage of material success.

But just ask sincere social workers or others who devote their lives to giving love, especially those who lack it themselves. They will tell you about the great personal happiness they feel from the ongoing love they share, regardless of anything they themselves may lack in life.

And it's not just due to the fact that social workers are often around people less fortunate than themselves, although that can surely help them to be happier with their own portions in life. It is mostly because they can see the difference their love makes in the lives of others, and because of the love and appreciation they feel in return.

If you examine carefully what kind of happiness material success brings, you will notice that it tends to be rather superficial. Fame and fortune might bring a lot of positive attention and create new opportunities in life, but not usually eternal ones. Even something as basic as giving charity can become a procedure that ends up dehumanizing it to a large degree.

Bringing many strangers into a charitable person's life can be emotionally overwhelming. It can become so distracting that it interferes with one's emotional flow, making it even harder to love and be loved. Money has never been the root of evil, but it certainly makes it difficult for people to be their spiritual best. Even the Talmud asserts this.[1]

It's probably been said at least a million times, if not more: We live to love and to be loved. Not just because it confirms that we exist and have some worth—though that never hurts—but because we were made in the image of God, and God is loving. When people love for that reason, it is the sweetest love of all, both to give and receive.

---

[1] Brochos 5b.

If that is true of love between people, it is even more true between people and God. Human love is limited and often gets distorted. Sincere people also have inner needs, many of which they may not be aware of but which affect their behavior toward others, especially people they care about. It is very hard to have pure love between humans.

This is why the Mishnah, when discussing such a high level of love, ignores the classic male-female relationship for a male-male relationship:

> All love that depends on a something, [when the] thing ceases, [the] love ceases; and [all love] that does not depend on anything will never cease. What is an example of love that depended on something? The love of Amnon for Tamar. And what is an example of love that did not depend on anything? The love of Dovid and Yonason. (Pirkei Avos 5:16; 5:19 in some versions)

We can assume that Avraham loved Sarah in the purest way possible. Nevertheless, he was a man and she was a woman, and God Himself made us with an attraction toward the other. It's not something we can really control.

Dovid's love for Yonason could supersede the physical aspects that can increase a person's attraction to someone else and create an ulterior motive for the relationship. Dovid loved Yonason and Yonason loved Dovid because of the virtue each displayed. In a sense they looked past each other and loved the virtue of the other. It doesn't get much better than that!

But that has limitations too because humans have limitations. We talk about boundless love, but the truth is that the only one who can actually back up such a claim is God. He is UNLIMITED, which makes HIS love unlimited as well.

It's like a bottomless well. The greater the capacity of people to feel God's love, the more they will feel it. If they were to feel more of God's love than they were capable of handling, they would die, albeit in ecstasy.

That is what God was telling Moshe when He said:

> You will not be able to see My face, for man shall not see Me and live. (Shemos 33:20)

There is a lot of discussion as to what this verse really means, since God doesn't have a face. Basically, to understand God as profoundly as Moshe Rabbeinu wanted would have resulted in his receiving more divine light than his body could handle. It would have been death by neshikah, divine kiss.

For anyone who dies that way, death is blissful. For Moshe Rabbeinu it would have also been premature, so his request was not fulfilled, at least not to the extent that he wished. He saw only the back of God's head, so to speak.

It is interesting that such a high level of divine light is called neshikah–kiss, a word always viewed as a sign of affection and love. Why would revelation of God be associated with love from God? Because they are one and the same, and not just between God and man, but between people as well.

It is not uncommon for someone to see them as two separate things—the person as distinct from the love that is felt and projected. In truth they are the same. It is impossible to be in touch with your ESSEN-TIAL self and not feel and give love, while it is impossible to love and not reveal your essential self.

That's why TRUE love is so liberating. When a person loves someone or even something for the right reasons, it feels AMAZING. It is UPLIFTING. And it brings the person PEACE. All this is the pleasure one receives from just being who he is in essence.

This is one of the greatest ironies of life and con jobs of the yetzer hara. Billions of people have lived during millennia with the belief that following the soul only leads to denial of pleasure. Material pleasure, they thought, is where life is lived to its fullest. Spiritual pleasure to many is pretty much an oxymoron.

If they only knew. If they only knew that pleasure they get from the physical world is possible only because of the spiritual one. If they could just realize that by turning physical pleasures into spiritual ones, the pleasure would not only increase, but last…and last… and last.

You can take the person out of the soul, and the yetzer hara is a master at that. But you can't take the soul out of the person, not without killing him. So as long as a person is alive, his soul lives inside the body, giving him life and driving him through it.

If people choose to ignore their souls, or even deny their existence, the joke is on them, and it is a bad one. The very source of their ultimate pleasure is locked away as they go off in pursuit of what they think is ultimate pleasure. They seek love and yet ignore the very basis of it. They yearn to be loved but disregard the very thing that attracts it to them.

One of the many fundamental differences between man and God is that God is pure. He has no mistaken thoughts, no misguided plans. He has not been damaged or misled by childhood experiences, and He has no need to hide behind facades to keep personal secrets from the outside world, all of which interferes with our ability to be our essential self.

God therefore is always purely Himself. And that is what He projects to the world. Even when He hides His face from man, it is a theatrical technique, not a shift in His "personality." God never changes, just the level of revelation of His light that He grants us.

That's why His love is so pure and awesome. Anyone who has been able to feel even a fraction of it has felt blessed beyond description. Anyone who knows God's love just a little cannot live without it. Just ask Dovid HaMelech who, through Tehillim, shared with history just how much God's love meant to him—everything.

In a sense our ability to feel God's love is a spiritual thermometer that tells us how much we are in touch with our essential self. This is basically what God was telling Kayin here:

> God said to Kayin, "Why are you annoyed, and why has your countenance fallen? Is it not that if you improve, you will be forgiven? If you do not improve, however, sin is lying at the entrance, and its longing is to you. But you can rule over it." (Bereishis 4:6-7)

This conversation took place right after God rejected Kayin's sacrifice, which made Kayin feel very unloved by God. His sacrifice was rejected because, after God blessed him with bounty, he showed his appreciation for that bounty by keeping the best of it for himself and returning to God the least of it. It was KAYIN'S spiritual outlook that set him up for divine rejection.

He became depressed about it as if he had done

no wrong. If we know we are to blame for our failure, why get angry at someone else? Kayin, spiritually out of touch, became depressed because he felt as if God had unjustly rejected his offering, and that he was being robbed of something to which he was entitled.

"Get back to your essential self," God told Kayin, "and you will figure it out and resume feeling My love for you. However," God warned him, "if you do not, and instead continue down this path, then you will add layers and layers of distance and will fall prey to your yetzer hara. You will have hatred instead of love, resentment instead of appreciation, and THEN you will become capable of the most despicable acts.

The bottom line is that self-rectification—the process of being in touch with your essential self and letting it lead—is the goal of life. We can measure our progress by how much of God's love we can feel. God is always transmitting His love. We just have to be on the right frequency to receive and notice it.

The culmination of this will be the Messianic Era. That is when the yetzer hara will be no more,[2] and we will be exactly who we are in essence. Therefore that is when we will feel God's love the most intensely. The daily pleasure will be unbelievable. But with a little bit of self-honesty and a desire to feel that love, we can enjoy some of it now.

---

[2] Succah 52a.

IMAGINE HEARING a voice in your head that says it is God speaking. "Don't worry," the voice assures you, "you're not going crazy. THIS is a REAL voice you're hearing in your head!"

Still not convinced, you ask for a sign, some kind of prediction to verify the divine origin of the voice, as you look for the phone number of a good psychiatrist, just in case. The voice makes a prediction and sure enough, the prediction comes true in a very convincing way. You accept that the voice is God's, and that you are now a prophet.

But then comes the command. The voice tells you to do something that goes against the wishes of society, and will be sure to make people question your sanity. If you tell them that God told you to do it, it will only confirm their suspicion that you are delusional. You will be isolated, cut off, and probably lose everything that is valuable to you.

So what do you do? You have no doubt that God spoke to you, but you can't prove it to anyone else. No one you care about will be prepared to just take your word for it and go along with you. Only you will know that what you are doing is the will of God.

Under such circumstances, how many people will rationalize away the voice? How many will listen to it and let happen whatever will happen?

Welcome to the world of Noach. This is what happened to him. God spoke to him and told him about the impending flood—only him and no one else. Then He commanded him to build an ark, and the entire society mocked him. Noach was lucky in that there was no insane asylum in those days.

But it is now more than 4,000 years later, and society is far different. It is bigger, a LOT bigger. It is a lot smarter too. The Western world is very sophisticated, quite scientific, and many people are either atheistic or agnostic. Insane asylums are readily available, and people who claim to hear from God usually end up in one of them. Even if they don't, they certainly end up on the fringes of society, and what rational person wants to live THERE?

But who cares? Compared to God, what does even the biggest society mean? God is the Creator, and society is only the created. HE knows the truth; they just THINK they do. It's what God thinks about you that counts most in life, not them, right?

Right. But that doesn't stop that little voice inside saying, "Are you nuts? People certainly will think you are! You'll lose everyone you love if you follow this voice. You'll be all alone. You'll lose all your credibility, and how can you survive without it? Can't you just get the voice to speak credibly to someone else to back you up?"

Do you feel it? Do you feel something like a massive wall inside? It's so big, so strong, and seemingly impenetrable. It's not made from stone or even wood. It's a psychological wall, built from fears we collected even before we could remember anything. Experiences have hurt us—or threatened to—and they became fears and part of our inner wall.

Like any wall, you may not notice it on a daily basis unless you have to get past it or keep something behind it. We tend to construct a life that safely avoids the wall. If we can't do that perfectly, we usually end up going into therapy or finding our own way to work through or around it. It is much easier to change the outside world than the inside one.

This inner psychological wall gets in the way and is the reason for many divorces—actual or psychological—between spouses, business partners, or friends. People can work together as long as they feel safe.

Threaten that safety, and they will feel that their walls are under siege and in need of protection. This is something people defend with their lives.

The problem, however, is not the wall. It is human nature to have one, part of our innate survival instinct. The problem is the material used to build it. If fears are justified, then the wall is justified. If it is built from false fears, then the wall becomes a false reality and will cause us to react to challenges in life in meaningless and usually destructive ways.

For example, if you knew God spoke to you and believed it with all your heart, nothing else should matter. People are temporary. Life is temporary. Humiliation is temporary. But the World-to-Come—where a person goes for listening to God—is ETERNAL, and will make all suffering in this world worth it.

All people really want to know and NEED to know at the end of the day is that they followed the truth, ultimately doing the right thing. It isn't always pleasant and can demand great sacrifice. But the people who are willing to make the sacrifice are the true heroes of society, and get not only our admiration but God's.

In the Messianic Era this will no longer be an issue. At some point near the beginning of it, the yetzer hara will be removed from mankind, rendering us incapable of any false values. The only thing we will believe in and follow will be the truth, GOD'S truth.[1] Tell people then that God spoke to you and they will envy and respect you in a soul-like way.

The problem is the world as it presently exists. Religious belief is unpopular and often mistaken. It has evolved with the times, and the times have not evolved in a spiritual manner. Rather than society adapting itself to religion, religion has adapted to the demands of secular society.

The rabbis warned against this more than 1500 years ago:

> During the generation that Ben Dovid will come…the wisdom of scholars will be diminished, and sin-fearing people will be despised. The face of the generation will be like the face of a dog, and the truth will be lacking, as it says: "And the truth is lacking, and he who departs from evil is negated" [Yeshayah 59:15]…"And he who departs from evil is negated?" The study hall of Rebi Sheila explained: Anyone who will deviate from evil will be deemed insane by people. (Sanhedrin 97a)

This makes standing up for truth very difficult to do, impossible for some. Few seem willing to make

---

[1] Succah 52a; Zechariah 14:9.

the supreme personal sacrifice that is required. But that doesn't mean that people who won't—or can't—don't beat themselves up over it. When our soul meets our wall, we suffer.

Noach certainly did in his time and Avraham in his. Many of their students have done so over the ages. But while others went in one direction or another to protect their walls, Noach and Avraham scaled theirs instead. They built a ladder from THEIR love of God and used it to scale the walls blocking God's love for them.

They are the REAL heroes of history, and they understood something that others did not. They knew that life—in all its glory and with all it has to give a person—was still no match for but a single moment of the love of God.

As hard or as impossible that is to believe, it is true. We look at the story of Rebi Akiva being tortured by the Romans,[2] and see HIS love of God. Saying Shema at the right time, while being tortured? Ecstatic that he can finally give up his life for God? You might think he was a religious fanatic, but you can't say that HE didn't love God completely!

But where was the love of God for Rebi Akiva at that horrible time? Even the angels questioned the means of his death and had to be silenced, even

---

[2] See Chapter One.

threatened by God. If anything, it looked as if God had pulled back completely from Rebi Akiva, leaving him to die a horrible death in God's Name—alone.

But not if you were to ask Rebi Akiva. He was the only one who could know otherwise, because he was the only one there who was capable of feeling the most intense love of God possible to be felt in this world, on this side of history. "Even now?" his students asked him. They meant that "even now you feel love of God?" His answer, given by the way he died while saying "echad" was "now more than ever!"

When Rebi Akiva started his climb toward Torah greatness, he was at the other extreme of the spiritual continuum. As he professed one day, he would have bitten the limb of a Torah scholar had one passed near him.[3] That was not at all the behavior of one who feels the love of God.

Eighty years later he himself was that Torah scholar. Whatever wall had been standing between him and God was gone, allowing him to become completely unafraid of doing what God wanted, even if others considered it crazy or even seditious. As the Talmud says elsewhere, people and their ways of thinking are temporary. Torah is eternal.[4]

---

[3] Pesachim 49b.

[4] Kesuvos 3b.

Many have claimed in one way or another to be God's warriors in this world. But they capitulated when faced with humiliation or, even worse, turned against God when they felt abandoned by Him. They had walls that blocked the love God had for them, giving them a sense of abandonment.

Chanina ben Teradyon was not like that. His story in the Talmud is even more moving than that of Rebi Akiva:

> They [the Romans] found Rebi Chanina ben Teradyon sitting and busy with Torah, publicly gathering assemblies [against their decrees]… Immediately they took him, wrapped him in the Sefer Torah, placed bundles of branches around him, and set them on fire. They then brought tufts of wool soaked in water and placed them over his heart so that he would not die quickly.
>
> His daughter cried, "Father, that I should see you in this state!"
>
> He replied, "If I alone were being burned, it would be too hard to bear. But now that I am burning together with the Sefer Torah, He who will respond to the disgrace of the Torah will respond to my disgrace as well."
>
> "Rebi," his students asked, "what do you see?"
>
> He answered them, "Parchment burning but

letters soaring heavenward."

"Open your mouth so that the fire can enter you!" they pleaded with him.

He replied, "Let Him who gave me [my soul] take it away, but one should not hurt himself."

The Roman executioner, [awed by his attitude at such a time] said, "Rebi, if I raise the flame and take away the tufts of wool from over your heart, will you bring me to eternal life?"

"Yes," he replied.

"Swear to me."

He swore to him. He raised the flame and removed the tufts of wool from over his heart, and his soul quickly departed. The executioner then threw himself into the fire. A heavenly voice exclaimed, "Rebi Chanina ben Teradyon and the executioner are [both] going to eternal life." (Avodah Zarah 18a)

The same thing has happened before and since then. An enemy of the Jewish people, even a murderous one, changed his mind and not only turned in favor of the Jewish people, but even become one of them.[5] This account of Rebi Chanina ben Teradyon's executioner is one of the most remarkable of all.

Why did he bother? It's not as if the Jewish peo-

____

5 Sanhedrin 96b.

ple got the upper hand and he was afraid of retribution. On the contrary, his Roman bosses, every bit as murderous as he was, were right behind him and willing to pay him in kind for shortening the show and showing mercy to a "worthless Jew" and enemy of the state!

What did the Roman executioner witness that so overwhelmed him that the other pressing issues were irrelevant to him? After all, jumping into a fire to end one's life is NOT the most pleasant way to go out! Just imagine the kind of teshuvah he had to do ON THE SPOT to go from being a vicious Roman executioner to a ben Olam HaBa, one destined for the World-to-Come. HIS wall sure came down in a hurry!

As an executioner, he had seen many people tortured to death, most of whom, including Jews, probably pleaded for their lives and acted in completely desperate ways. Faced with death, and usually a prolonged and painful one, they just didn't have the wherewithal to suffer silently, as if unmoved from their past level of belief. All of a sudden their relationship with God seemed to vanish in their final moments.

Rebi Chanina was what is called the "real deal." A person's belief is only as strong as he is willing to stay with it as conditions worsen and make it difficult to do so. Rebi Chanina not only didn't snap, but he went out calmly, with dignity, with LOVE OF GOD.

It is always better to live for God than to have to

die for Him. Death is a one-time opportunity to sanctify His great and holy Name. Life provides opportunity after opportunity to do so. We weren't created to die, but ever since leaving paradise, it became a necessary part of life, for the sake of ETERNAL life.

On the other hand, because death is a one-time deal, it is the best way to show just how strongly a person feels about the principles that led to death. The stakes can't get any higher, and the more willing a person is at the moment of truth, the stronger his belief appears.

So what was Rebi Chanina really exhibiting by his incredibly heroic death for the sake of God and Torah? How does one do such a thing if he does not truly love God with all he is and has? And who loves God with all he is and has if he does not feel loved by God to the same extent, if not more? And who watching that would not, all of a sudden, want to feel the same way?

Like Noach in his time, Avraham in his, and Rebi Akiva, Rebi Chanina had no wall between him and God. He had felt God's intense love for him throughout his life, and now it calmed him during his moments before death.

And as Rebi Akiva explained to his students at the very end, this is not something you can just draw on at the last minute. Getting to a point where you can know such an intense love from God is a work in progress, spanning your entire life. It's a life's work to take down that wall, hidden inside, that took so long to build.

But it is more than worth it. The love of God waiting on the other side of the wall is beyond comprehension. People kill themselves for physical pleasures, even coming up with the expression "to die for" something. And yet those pleasures are temporal and incredibly limiting, as they themselves are limited. That is why the people who pursue them have to keep coming back for more, and more, and more.

Not God's love for us, though. Once accessed, it never stops flowing. It courses spiritually through us, providing vitality, both spiritual and physical, and the opportunity for a higher dimension to life. So get out the hammer and chisel. There's a wall waiting to come down.

THERE ARE SEVERAL stages to loving children. When they are first born, we can't seem to love them enough. When they start to become mischievous, it seems cute as long as they don't do any real damage. When they learn the word "no," we start to get frustrated with them, and when they begin to act out, we show anger.

Some kids grow up nicely, but others develop selfish tendencies, which does not endear them to us, sometimes for many years. When they become teenagers and learn what independence really means, a parent can start to feel as if old age is accelerating faster than normal. Some children and parents never really resolve their differences.

The child blames the parent. The parent blames

the child. Between the two of them, their love may fall through the cracks. Children seem to believe that parents OWE them a living, and parents feel that children owe them FOR their living. Resentment can easily shut the heart of each to the other.

And as each side justifies its dislike of the other, both hurt inside. They cry inside. They can be 80-years-old and 60-years-old, respectively, but they still cry inside, sometimes even on the outside. Parents were created to love their kids, and children were created to love their parents. It's the most natural relationship in the world, and when it doesn't function right, it's the most UNNATURAL thing in the world.

And yet it is incredibly common—in the secular world. You can criticize the Torah world for a lot of things, and people do. But one thing is for certain—it does a better job at educating children to be decent people than the secular world does. And the secular world can't disagree with that, not statistically and certainly not in terms of programming, which in the secular world doesn't include development of middos.[1]

To begin with, the fifth of the Ten Commandments is to honor and fear your parents. That means different things to children at different ages. But everyone knows that the day will come when children can no longer be easily coerced by their parents, and

---

[1] Character traits, especially gratitude and humility.

they will either have sincere respect and love for them or they won't.

It's a two-pronged approach. A Torah education is supposed to help children grow up to be more self-less, with ultimately meaningful values. If they follow the program, they will emerge to be more or less responsible and caring adults. If they don't, they will not be much different from those in the non-Torah world beyond them.

At the same time, parents are also supposed to grow up. Just as the Torah commands children to respect their parents, the parents are commanded to be worthy of respect. There are halachos that impose such respect on children regardless of much of their parents' behavior, but the Torah also knows that children cannot respect abusive parents.

Where is a parent commanded by the Torah to be worthy of respect? In many places, from mitzvos to be like God[2] to those that teach us to love our neighbor as ourself.[3] Just as we would want our parents to be worthy of our respect, so do our children want us to be worthy of theirs. As Hillel said, "Don't do to others what you do not want done to you."[4]

Parent-child relationships are remarkably different

---

[2] Devarim 28:9.

[3] Vayikra 19:18.

[4] Shabbos 30a.

from all others. There is no wall present, so the love just flows between them. Children feel the love of parents and usually can't do enough to show that they feel the same way. The bond is one of the deepest possible and goes beyond the physical limitations of this world. And more than likely, it is one that will get passed down from one generation to the next, a truly marvelous and gratifying accomplishment.

And that is only talking about human relationships—between human parents and children. Some parents, however, fail their children. They have their own issues that can interfere with family relationships. They can even act in despicable ways and be incapable of exhibiting love to their children.

God is obviously vastly different. He is our Father and we are His children. He is the PERFECT father though we be His imperfect children. His love is continuous for us, though ours for Him falters and often withers. There is never a time when He does not deserve our respect. If we think there is, it is from our shortsightedness, not from a lack of caring on God's part.

You can't always be sure with human parents. They can love their children tremendously but get so distracted by life they forget to show it. Parents know they love their children, but children, lacking obvious signs, may question it.

Or parents can misread a child's aloofness as in-

dependence, and only later find out it was estrange-
ment. "You never showed me you cared," the adult
child complains to an older parent. "You don't know
how much I wanted to!" the parent defends. "But I
thought you wanted space, so I backed off."

God is one parent, however, who can read our
heart. He knows what we're thinking even when we
don't, and knows what is best for us even when we
think otherwise. You can't make a human parent love a
child. You don't have to make a parent love a child
when that parent is God.

PURIM IS THE most curious holiday of the Jewish yearly cycle. It can certainly be the most fun. Rabbinic in origin to commemorate the miraculous victory of Mordechai and Esther over Haman in 353 BCE, it lacks the halachic seriousness of Torah holidays like Pesach, Shavuos, and Succos. The mitzvos we do perform are the kind that just about everyone looks forward to, especially the mishteh–drinking feast.

If you ask someone familiar with all the Jewish holidays to list them in order of holiness, Purim would certainly not be at the top—not even close. It may be a HOLIDAY, but it is not a HOLY day in the minds of most people. Some people dress like clowns. Many others get drunk to the point that they act like clowns.

What about the fact that the rabbis say that Yom

HaKippurim, the holiest day of the year, can be read as Yom k'Purim—a day LIKE Purim? Doesn't that make Purim HOLIER than Yom Kippur? "Ahhh, that's just to make sure you behave yourself on a day the rabbis know people don't!"

Kabbalists know differently:

> Hence when it says that in the future…all holidays will no longer exist except for Purim and Yom HaKippurim, it is referring to the time of resurrection, 40 years after Kibbutz Golios—ingathering of the exiles—until the end of the 214 years… (Drushei Olam HaTohu, Chelek 2, Drush 4, Anaf 12, Siman 10)

This is Kabbalah and requires explanation. It will be somewhat of an intellectual journey, so we'll discuss it in sections.

Olam HaZeh–This World

The first thing to point out is that history consists of different time periods. There is Olam HaZeh–this world, which for all intents and purposes began with Creation itself, even though life in paradise was on a much higher spiritual plane than it is now. This time is principally the one in which man has a yetzer hara—evil inclination. Evil can exist and free will is possible.

Thus it is the only period of history during which

people can make choices that can either earn them reward in Olam HaBa–the World to Come or reduce it. Personal choices—even the decision not to choose —result in rectification of self and world or detract from both.

Yemos HaMoshiach–Messianic Era

At some point seemingly known only to God, Moshiach will come and bring an end to history as we know it. He will lead the war against evil and herald a new era of history referred to in the verse "God will be King over all the land, and on that day God will be One and His Name will be One."[1]

The threshold to this utopian era was spoken about by the prophets and referred to as the War of Gog and Magog. By the time it is over, evil will be gone from the world and no one will ever again question the existence of God or validity of Torah. The yetzer hara will be completely eliminated and all human vices will belong to the past.[2]

All remaining Jews in the Diaspora will return to Israel, the Temple will return to Har Moriah in Jerusalem, and the entire world will yearn for closeness to God. The world will function as it has for thou-

---

[1] Zechariah 14:9.

[2] Succah 52a; Drushei Olam HaTohu, Chelek 2, Drush 4, Anaf 12, Siman 10.

sands of years but with each passing day life will become more miraculous and less natural.[3]

Moshe Rabbeinu, Moshiach in his time, walked the earth for 79 years until he was called by God to free the Jewish people; he was 80 years old at the time of the redemption. That Messianic Era technically began with his birth, even though the Jewish people suffered tremendously until he finally freed them.

Likewise, the first stage of the final Messianic Era at the End-of-Days will begin well in advance of Moshiach's actual revelation. History will again seem to get worse before it gets better, but this will all be part of the messianic process leading to the final stage of a world free of the yetzer hara. It is all for the purpose of bringing us to the next stage of history and world perfection.

Techiyas HaMeisim—Resurrection of the Dead

Even though the yetzer hara will be long gone by the end of Yemos HaMoshiach, man's physical features will not be. They too will have to change for man to go to Olam HaBah, the World-to-Come, a completely spiritual reality.

Kabbalah teaches that the first man was not created on the same level of physicality as we are. His

---

[3] Brochos 34b; Drushei Olam HaTohu, Chelek 2, Drush 4, Anaf 12, Siman 9.

body was more like a soul and only became physical as a result of the sin. Likewise, the world of which he was a part went through a similar transformation.[4] This is the world with which we are familiar.

In order for people to revert to the original pre-sin state of man, they will have to die and be resurrected free from all spiritual impurities. This process is called Techiyas HaMeisim, or the resurrection of the dead, and all those who go through it will return to the world more like angels than the people we are used to.[5]

This process of resurrection will not only rectify mankind, but all physical existence as well. According to the Zohar, it will take either 210 years or 214 years to complete, since people will die and be resurrected at different times. Exactly when people will die and return like angels will depend on their personal merit.

By year 6,000 from Creation,[6] the last person will have died and been resurrected, concluding the period of history called Olam HaZeh—this world. At that time the world will have become completely spiritual, ascending to the level of the first stage of Olam HaBah. It is to this 214 years of history that the following refers:

---

[4] Drushei Olam HaTohu, Drush Aitz HaDa'as, Siman 3-7.
[5] Drushei Olam HaTohu, Chelek 2, Drush 4, Anaf 12, Siman 9.
[6] Sanhedrin 97a.

At that time a great change will occur to the entire world, even to those still existing in this world, although they will remain quite physical. At the present time the world consists of three categories: impure, pure, and holy, and even the pure of today is still quite profane, lacking holiness. However, at that time everything will be on the level of pure and holy. It is with respect to this time that they say that all the holidays will no longer apply, for all days will have the holiness of the holidays; profane days will no longer exist... (Drushei Olam HaTohu, Chelek 2, Drush 4, Anaf 12, Siman 10)

A Jewish holiday is more than just a commemoration of a past event. The redemption-like event that originally occurred, which led to the establishment of the holiday, was the result of a specific energy that became accessible at that time. By responding to the events of their day in a way that God approved, the Jewish people of that time were allowed to access this level of light and miraculously to succeed.

Once the specific light was discovered at a specific time of the year, the Torah marked the time with a holiday. This was a way to make sure that future generations remained aware of the spiritual opportunity of that time, and to use it whenever that time came around again. When a holiday ends, so does its opportunity, since its entire light does not belong to this period of history, but rather to a future, holier one.

There are different holidays because there are different facets of God's light. One aspect is the basis of the holiday of Pesach. Another is the basis of the holiday of Shavuos, and another of the holiday of Succos, etc. The same thing is true of the rabbinic holidays of Purim and Chanukah, their lights having been revealed after the Torah had been recorded.

Apparently the lights of Pesach, Shavuos, Succos, Shemini Atzeres, Rosh Chodesh, and Rosh Hashanah belong to the period of Techiyas HaMeisim. Therefore during that time special days of the year will not be necessary to access them, and the holidays which granted access to their lights on this side of history will no longer be necessary.

> However, Purim and Yom HaKippurim will not be annulled at that time, since Purim is the revelation of the Yesod of Abba, as it is known in Kavanos Purim. Therefore it alludes to the eighth millennium when Chochmah will be the primary influence. (Drushei Olam HaTohu, Chelek 2, Drush 4, Anaf 12, Siman 10)

The Hebrew word Yesod translates to foundation in English and Abba of course is father. But these words mean little unless people know something about the sefiros.

What are the sefiros? They are the spiritual system that God created to emanate His light to first make and then sustain Creation. There are 10 sefiros—Keser, Chochmah, Binah, Chesed, Gevurah, Tifferes, Netzach, Hod, Yesod, and Malchus—and each represents a particular aspect and strength of God's light. Each one contains ALL the various aspects of spiritual and physical Creation that were made and are maintained, as per the will of God.

And just as each sefirah is one of a system of 10, likewise each sefirah has its own personal set of 10 sefiros. They can be compared to family members who get married and have families of their own. For example Keser has its own Keser, Chochmah, Binah, etc.

What is relevant to this discussion is how particular sefiros are the basis for all that happens in their respective millennium. They are the cosmic DNA of history, making possible all that occurs. Thus for example the sefirah of Chesed was the energy for all that happened during the first 1,000 years, Gevurah was the energy for the events of the second 1,000 years, and so on.

Yesod is the basis for all that has happened and will happen in this sixth and final millennium of Olam HaZeh. It is also the only sefirah to have two parts aside from its subset of 10 sefiros. The first one corresponds to our stage of history and the second corresponds to the Messianic Era,[7] including Techiyas Ha-Meisim.

Then comes somewhat of a twist. The seventh millennium, which is already the first stage of Olam HaBah, corresponds to the sefirah of Malchus. But one would assume that since it is the lowest of the 10 sefiros, it should not correspond to a higher level of reality than its predecessors. But it does.

That is because the sefirah of Malchus is only temporarily at the bottom of the spiritual totem pole. By the time history reaches year 6,000, not only will Malchus be completely rectified, it will be elevated to a position even higher than the sefirah of Chesed—just below Binah. At that level in the sefiros, the World-to-Come actually begins.

At 7,000 the Malchus and its corresponding period of history will be complete, and the sefirah of Binah will take over for stage two of the World-to-Come.

> Likewise, Yom HaKippurim, which is the level of Binah, is the sod of the World-to-Come of the seventh millennium, the time called "the entire day is Shabbos"… (Drushei Olam HaTohu, Chelek 2, Drush 4, Anaf 12, Siman 10)

---

[7] Hakdamos uSha'arim, p. 172.

This is an amazing thing that we tend to take for granted. Even though Yom Kippur comes around once a year and is a fixed part of the yearly Jewish cycle, its light is actually otherworldly. When the door opens on Yom Kippur, the light of the second stage of the World-to-Come floods through for the person who takes proper spiritual advantage of the day.

As such, the 10th of Tishrei must be observed even in Techiyas HaMeisim in order to access its light at least once a year. We won't have to fast at that time or spend the whole day in prayer, but we will have to wait until that day of Yom Kippur to access the light of Binah.

When the seventh millennium begins, however, then it will be Yom Kippur every day, on a level of eternal pleasure we can't possibly fathom. It will be the last of the holidays to disappear, except for…of all things, the rabbinic holiday of Purim!

Even during this incredibly spiritual and holy time, when Yom Kippur will cease to be an independent holiday, Purim WILL be one. This one holiday—seemingly devoid of all holiness NOW—will be continue as a holiday beyond the period of the holiest day of the year, Yom Kippur, and on a level that is holier than our current ability to imagine! How can this be, and what does it say about Purim?

We have this question because we understand our world in kind of an upside-down way, thanks to the yetzer hara:

> Rav Yosef, the son of Rebi Yehoshua ben Levi, became ill and fell into a trance. When he recovered his father asked him, "What did you see?"
>
> "I saw an upside-down world," he answered. "Those who are above [in this world were] below [over there], and those who are below [in this world were] above [over there]."
>
> "My son," he told him, "you saw a clear world." (Pesachim 50a)

This is the only world we know. We're born into it and we die in it. We've heard that there was once a place called Gan Aiden, the Garden of Eden, and that it was a paradise. But since nothing in this world ever comes close to it, for us its reality is just a distant imagination.

It is, though, the world for which we were created. This one—in which people die, suffer, kill, get killed, eat, starve, become rich and poor, feel anger, jealousy, and a need for revenge—is just a passing one. Compared to the eternal one before and after, it will have been barely a moment in time. But meanwhile it seems to go on and on and on.

With a yetzer hara we are trained to seek physical comfort and avoid pain, to pursue materialism and shun spirituality. The former feels natural while the latter takes a lot of training and almost supernatural inner resolve. It's not that science has proven that religion is irrelevant—which it can't do. It is that people use science as a justification to turn their backs on the spiritual world they fear will deny them quality of life.

The individuals are rare, even among the religious, who have learned the opposite and believe it. They are part of the fortunate few who have seen past the machinations of their yetzer haras and the trickery of the Sitra Achra, aka Satan. They have opted out of the conspiracy that has overtaken vast parts of the human world and activity, and instead refine themselves spiritually, removing their walls, brick by spiritual brick, to bask in the love of God.

As we are supposed to do on Purim. Purim is a holiday of da'as Elohim, mentioned here:

> If you want it like money and pursue it like treasures, then you will understand fear of God, and da'as Elohim you will find. (Mishlei 2:4-5)

> Kabbalistically wine really refers to the same thing.

> Rebi Chanina said: Anyone who becomes settled through wine has the da'as of his Creator…

(Eiruvin 65a)[8]

How the two, da'as and wine, are similar is less of an issue in this discussion than how they accomplish the same thing. Whether through da'as Elohim or through wine, the goal of neutralizing the body and freeing the soul can be achieved. Rebi Chanina said nothing about drinking to the point of a drunken stupor, at which point people may act in a quite soulless manner. He spoke about becoming settled, to the point that people can finally merit the da'as of their Creator.

Torah can and should do the same thing. If people are learning Torah as deeply as possible, plumbing its infinite depths to the best of their ability in search of an increasingly more profound understanding of life, they will find da'as Elohim and peace of soul:

> A person who only performs mitzvos [only] merits the Nefesh…If he makes additional effort to learn Torah, learning it, thinking about it, and constantly teaching the Oral Law, always learning it for its own sake, then he will merit the Ruach…If the person makes additional effort and

---

[8] See my books "Redemption to Redemption" and "Purim Lite" for a more detailed discussion.

learns…the secrets of the Torah, he will also merit the Neshamah…The Neshamah will give off light in the Ruach within him and will add level to level, wisdom to wisdom, and he will then be called an adam shalaim—complete person, regarding whom it says: "God made man in His image" (Bereishis 1:26).

It's not that Purim doesn't have any serious mitzvos. It's that Purim doesn't NEED any serious mitzvos. Regarding the other holidays, including Yom Kippur, we need to do their mitzvos just to line ourselves up with their portals of light and to make use of them. On Purim the light is so high up, so sublimely powerful, that people need only spiritual focus to bask in it and experience a level of the next world's divine love, Purim love, unparalleled on any other holiday of the Jewish year.

So of course Purim is also the most distracting holiday of the year. It is the death of the yetzer hara, which will do anything it can to prevent people from accessing the light of Purim. It knows instinctively that people exposed to such a high level of divine light will scale walls just to experience the divine love on the other side:

God said to Moshe [at Mt. Sinai], "Go down, warn the people lest they break [their formation to go nearer] to God, to see, and many of them will fall." (Shemos 19:21)

"Warn" them not to go up the mountain, "lest they break" their position because of their longing for God, to see [Him], and they move too close to the side of the mountain, "and many of them will fall." (Rashi)

Hence the holiday of Purim is also compared to the giving of Torah, even considered to be its actual conclusion more than 1,000 years later.[9] Mt. Sinai was the scene of a unique unity of the Jewish people,[10] and Purim has mitzvos to seek the same level of achdus–unity. Da'as is the koach hachibur, the power to unify.[11] Just as it did so at the giving of Torah, it can do it again every Purim.

It is not Purim, therefore, that lacks holiness. It is the person who can't see its incredible holiness who lacks it. This has been the principle of God's light since the first day of Creation:

God saw that the light was good, and God separated between the light and the darkness.

____

9 Shabbos 86a.
10 Rashi, Shemos 19:2.
11 See Chapter 2.

(Bereishis 1:4)

He saw that the wicked were unworthy of using it, and therefore set it apart for the righteous in the future time. (Rashi)

He made a separation in the illumination of the light, that it should not flow or give off light except for the righteous, whose actions draw it down and make it shine. However, the actions of the evil block it, leaving them in darkness, and this itself was the hiding of the light. (Sefer HaKlallim, Klal 18, Anaf 8, Os 4)

Light, love…it's the same thing here. And it is also the TRUE simchah–joy we wish people when saying "Purim samayach." We're really saying this: "May you merit to access this high level light of the World-to-Come, and enjoy the intense love of God and all the good that it brings."

CHANUKAH IS ON the other side of the "cohen"[1] from Purim. In many respects it is a much quieter holiday, with its only mitzvah being to light the menorah each of the eight nights of the holiday. Latkes and doughnuts are purely optional and bad for your health, but they make the holiday much more delicious. Playing dreidel provides fun.

You may have noticed in the previous chapter that Chanukah was not mentioned as one of the holidays that will cease to be observed at some time in the future. In fact Chanukah was not mentioned at all.

---

[1] Yes, it should be "coin." But Chanukah was a victory achieved by kohanim, descendants of Aharon HaKohen who were THE prime example of love of God, and what it means to be inspired by it. Hence, the pun.

Given that it is specifically a holiday of light, shouldn't we know WHICH light? What spiritual portal opens for us during the eight days of Chanukah?

Chanukah emphasizes something that we don't really focus on from day to day—the idea of chayn, the word formed by the first two letters of Chanukah, Ches and Nun. Some read the word Chanukah as Ches-Nun—chayn Vav-Chof-Heh—and 25. That is, there was chayn on the 25th day of Kislev, and it led to the miracles of Chanukah.

But what IS chayn?

Usually translated as grace, this word is used primarily to mean something like congeniality. But the first time the Torah uses the word chayn is here, in reference to Noach, and more importantly, explains why he survived the Great Flood:

> And God said, "I will blot out man, whom I created, from the face of the earth, from man to cattle to creeping things, to the fowl of the heavens, for I regret that I made them." But Noach found CHAYN in the eyes of God. (Bereishis 6:7- 8)

From these verses it does not seem as if congeniality quite fits as a definition of chayn. God was angry at that time, prepared to wipe out mankind, and Noach was saved because he was a nice guy? Hard to imagine, which makes it seem as if there must be more to chayn than meets the eye.

Whatever chayn is, it has to be central to the master plan for Creation. God is single-minded, in a godly kind of way. He is only interested in ONE thing, and never gets distracted from it. He made the world for a specific reason, to accomplish a specific purpose. Good is anything that helps Creation achieve that purpose, and the more good something does, the better, the more godly, the more REDEEMING it is.

Countless Torah books describe the purpose of Creation and many stories illustrate it. One particular account from the Talmud basically says it all, eloquently. It is the story of Elazar ben Durdaya, a terrible sinner who at the last minute woke up just in time to do teshuvah for all his terrible sins.

> He went out, sat down between two hills and mountains, and shouted, "Hills and mountains, plead for mercy for me!"
>
> They answered, "How can we pray for you? We are in need of mercy ourselves, as it says, 'For the mountains shall depart and the hills be removed!'" [Yeshaya 54:10].
>
> So he shouted, "heaven and earth, plead for mercy for me!"
>
> But they too answered back, "How can we? We are in need of mercy ourselves, as it says, 'For the heavens shall vanish like smoke, and the

earth shall wax old like a garment'" [Yeshaya 51:6].

He then called out, "Sun and moon, plead for mercy for me!"

But they too said, "How can we pray for you? We need it ourselves, as it says, 'Then the moon will be confounded and the sun ashamed'" [Yeshaya 24:3].

So he called out [one last time], "Stars and constellations, plead for mercy for me!"

But they responded, "How can we pray for you? We are in need of it ourselves, as it says, 'And all the hosts of heaven shall decay'" [Yeshaya 34:4].

He [then] said, "The matter therefore depends on me alone!"

He put his head between his knees and cried out in a loud voice until he died. A heavenly voice proclaimed, "Rebi Elazar Ben Durdaya is destined for the life of the World-to-Come!"

Rebi[2] wept and said, "One can acquire the World-to-Come after many years, and another [person can do it] in a [single] moment!...And not only are repentants accepted [by heaven], they are even called 'rebi.'" (Avodah Zarah 17a)

---

2 Rebi Yehudah HaNasi, the redactor of the Mishnah.

It is a remarkable story for several reasons. Just the way that Rebi Elazar, in the midst of yet another terrible sin, could wake up to his predicament and, seemingly on a dime, go in the opposite spiritual direction, is amazing. Most people in such a bad state are too far gone to be impacted by any inner spiritual voice, let alone run to do teshuvah.

Another remarkable aspect is how the student became the teacher. The story attaches the appellation rebi to his name at death. Through his supreme act of teshuvah, he went from being simply Elazar ben Durdaya to being REBI Elazar ben Durdaya. Apparently what he did has something to teach ALL of us about life, even those who devote their lives to pursuing the path of Torah.

It probably has something to do with this curious statement:

> In the place the repentant stands, even the completely righteous cannot stand. (Brochos 34b)

This is somewhat counterintuitive. Unquestionably a sinner who repents is to be put on a pedestal and praised. But that's similar to having your cake and eating it too, whereas the righteous person who has been that way through his entire journey is as pure as they come. Doesn't it make sense that such a person should be more spiritually advanced than someone who lived a life of sin, only to later rectify himself?

Yes and no.

There is an expression that says "there is nothing worse than reformed sinners." Why? They tend to become zealous in the other direction, making sinners feel terrible about their sinful ways and Torah-observant Jews feel as if they are not taking their mitzvos seriously enough.

While that is often the case, the truth is that from God's perspective, there is little BETTER than a reformed sinner. But don't get the idea that you should go out and sin with the intention of later doing teshuvah! Adam HaRishon tried that and it didn't go over well with God. The Talmud says that it doesn't work anyhow.[3] It's talking about people who intended to lead sinful lives and only later came to their senses—like Rebi Elazar ben Durdaya—and then did teshuvah.

What's the big deal?

Just ask Noach, whose name is the reverse of the word chayn. He was at odds with his entire generation, which mocked his way of life. The people had basically adopted a lifestyle to "Eat, drink, and be merry, because what else is there to do?" Noach took the opposite approach and exercised material restraint in order to promote spiritual growth. In other words, others of his generation were BODY-driven but

---

[3] Yoma 85b.

he was SOUL-driven.

The differences between these approaches to life are obvious in many ways. But the main difference is belief in God and the pursuit of a relationship with Him. This is the point of life, and the soul is the means of achieving it. Someone who doesn't believe he has a soul certainly won't go looking for it, so how could he possibly live by it?

When a person does make his soul a priority, he empowers it. He gives it greater ability to be part of the decision-making process, which will dictate his direction in life. And as the soul increases in expression, the body too becomes impacted by its light to the point that it can no longer block it, and it radiates to the outside. THAT'S what people see when they sense the chayn of someone.

No one displays this more clearly than a ba'al teshuvah, a repentant sinner. Why would anyone in his right mind go from living the life of a body, which is mitzvah-free, to a life filled with mitzvos? There are only two possibilities. Either he lost his mind or…discovered something that convinced him it was to his personal benefit to make the change to a more spiritual lifestyle.

We call that the soul.

That is the deeper meaning of this idea:

These [letters Yud and Heh refer to the] two

worlds that the Holy One, Blessed Is He, created, one with [the letter] Heh and one with [the letter] Yud. I do not know whether the World-to-Come [was created] with [the letter] Yud and this world [was created] with [the letter] Heh, or whether this world [was created] with [the letter] Yud and the World-to-Come [was created] with [the letter] Heh.

But when [the verse] says that "these are the generations of the heaven and of the earth when they were created—behibare'am" [Bereishis 2:4], do not read behibare'am [when they were created], but rather beHEH bera'am [He created them with the letter Heh]. And why was this world created with [the letter] Heh? Because [the letter Heh], which [is open on its bottom] is similar to a portico, [which is open on one side; it alludes to this world] where anyone who wishes to leave [that is, sin] may leave. Why is the [left] leg of [the Heh] suspended [and not joined to the roof of the letter]? So that if someone repents, he is brought [back] in [through the opening at the top]. (Menachos 29b)

Add the following two midrashim to the discussion, and the bottom line of life in this world becomes even clearer:

"Go and see the works of God, awesome in deed–alillah toward mankind." [Tehillim 66:5]. Go and see how when the Holy One, Blessed Is He, created the world, He created the Angel of Death on the first day as well…And yet, although man was created on the sixth day, death was blamed on him. To what is this similar? To a man who decided that he wanted to divorce his wife and wrote her a bill of divorce, after which he went home holding it, looking for a pretext–alillah to give it to her. He told her,

"Prepare me something to drink."

She did. He took it and said, "Here is your divorce."

She asked him, "Why?"

He told her, "Leave my house! You made me a warm drink."

So she asked, "Were you able to know that I would prepare you a warm drink in the future so that you wrote a bill of divorce in advance and came home with it?"

So too did Adam say to the Holy One, Blessed Is He, "Master of the Universe, the Torah was with You for 2,000 years before You created the world]…And what is written in it? 'This is the law when a man will die in a tent' [Bamidbar 19:14]. Now if You had not established death for Your creations, would You have written this? Rather

You just want to blame death on me! (Tanchuma, Vayaishev 4)

After Kayin killed his brother, Hevel, his father, Adam HaRishon, asked him, "What was your judgment?"

Kayin answered, "I did teshuvah, and the full impact of justice was not applied to me."

"Such is the power of teshuvah!" Adam exclaimed. "I did not realize that by doing teshuvah a person's past misdeeds are erased so completely that they are considered by God as if they had never taken place!" (Bereishis Rabbah 22:28)

Clearly this world was made for teshuvah. "But," you may ask, "if it were made for teshuvah, doesn't that imply that it was also made for sinning?" Nice try. The answer is a flat-out no, because you don't have to sin to do teshuvah. You just have to improve.

There is no greater improvement than that of a reformed sinner, and a simple analogy makes the point. If you light a match in a poorly lit room, it will be visible, but its impact will be minimal. But turn off the lights, which makes the room dark, and the match will appear like a torch!

Likewise, when a person already good goes from there to better, the improvement is great but not very visible on the outside. Some people might even miss it altogether, expecting such behavior from someone known to live a spiritually refined life.

But with someone who goes from sinner to tzaddik, the improvement can be shocking. When one very popular Israeli TV and movie personality did it, shock waves reverberated through the entire secular community. Some people even got depressed or worse.

It wasn't just that they lost a favorite entertainer. The world is filled with plenty of those. It was more that the star's choice to do teshuvah was a blatant and fearful statement against the very godless and materialistic world that his worshippers lived in. If HE could change his mind about a hedonistic lifestyle, perhaps they should too!

I don't know if many followed in his footsteps, the vast majority having written him off as a lunatic, just as people did in Noach's time. That was easier than facing a hard truth and making difficult changes. Few people are self-honest enough to go that route in such a situation.

The problem with REAL chayn is that when people don't have it, someone else's REALLY bothers them and makes them feel uncomfortable. In the presence of someone else's revealed soul, their own soul gets aroused, and that can be like a guilty conscience, a very foreign and often unwelcome feeling when you're not used to it.

There is a very important message in all this, and it is the basis for the holiday of Chanukah. It has to be remembered that Chanukah was the last holiday established before the Jewish people embarked on their fourth and final exile, with extreme hester panim—hiding of God's face. It was a love letter from God, that we can open each year on Chanukah to recall how to access His love, even in times as dark as ours, even with artificial lighting.

God stopped talking to us long ago. Even the righteous among us could not get any kind of direct message from God. Prophecy was long gone and the Jewish people seemed to be on their own. Emunah was all that carried Judaism from one generation to the next, especially when persecution made it next to impossible to live as a Torah Jew.

Chanukah reminded us that God has different ways of communicating with us. It can be direct, like it was between Adam HaRishon and God, and later between Moshe Rabbeinu and God. It can be through dreams, as it was for other prophets on a lesser level. And it can even be on the level called Ruach HaKodesh, which literally means holy spirit.

What is Ruach HaKodesh, if it is not direct prophecy, or dream-talk? What else is there?

There is the soul. Although we may seem to lose touch with God, our soul never does. It can't. It is a spark of divine light, a fragment of God's will. As long as we have a soul, we are in touch with God on some inner level. The reality of God is within us, as it says:

> And God created man in His image; in the image of God He created him… (Bereishis 1:27)

The problem is similar to what happens if someone puts a phone receiver inside layers of fabric. The more layers the voice has to penetrate, the less clear it will sound, until eventually it will be silenced completely. The person won't even know that someone phoned him.

The trouble is that many people live that way, including those who live by Torah. To live by Torah means to have fewer layers blocking the light of the soul, but there can still be enough for people not to be in touch with their souls. That's when Torah life becomes more habit than living.

The events of Chanukah bored through those layers and awoke the souls of Mattisyahu and his family. If they had been zealots before, they became super-zealots as a result. The light of their souls burst forth, bringing them to a higher level of existence that superseded the world of the Greeks and their Hellenist admirers.

It was a level on which miracle was nature, on which a handful of ill-equipped soldiers could defeat a well-seasoned large army, and one day's worth of oil could burn for eight days. And on that level people suddenly felt in touch with God in a way they hadn't previously known was possible, especially so late in history. THAT is the chayn in Chanukah.

And that is the chayn in teshuvah. The greater the teshuvah, the more the chayn. Teshuvah is soul-driven, so when people do it, their souls are revealed to the outside world. Like Chanukah, teshuvah brings the spiritual realm to the forefront, and puts people back in touch with God. In touch with their ruach–spirit which is kadosh–holy, they merit the direction of Ruach HaKodesh.

That is the best part. Ruach HaKodesh is just an-other name for the love of God. You can't be in touch with God and not feel His love. They are one and the same. Humans can love but hide it. God doesn't, as He informed Kayin:[4]

> God said to Kayin, "Why are you annoyed, and why has your countenance fallen? Is it not that if you improve, you will be forgiven? If you do not improve, however, sin is lying at the entrance, and its longing is to you, but you can rule over it." (Bereishis 4:6-7)

In other words, God told Kayin, "That sense of

---

[4] Mentioned in Chapter 4.

abandonment you feel? That's from you, not Me. Just get back in touch with your soul again, reveal your inner chayn on the outside, and notice how good you will feel about My love for you!"

This was and is Chanukah's message to all generations. Lighting the menorah tells us that just as we reveal the inner light of the olive by extracting it from deep within the olive, likewise must we extract our soul from within the depths of the body. Who doesn't feel the love of God when watching the menorah illuminate the darkness of night and recalling the miracles of days gone by? Who won't feel the love of God as his soul illuminates the world around him and shares its chayn with other souls?

We are at the end of history, at least as we know it. Prophecy is but an ancient idea, direct and indirect. But we still have our soul. We have the ability to do teshuvah and to mine our inner chayn, along with the light from which it draws.

What level of light is that?

The messianic light, which is why Chanukah will no longer need to be a unique period of time during the Messianic Era. With the yetzer hara gone, all the layers covering the soul will vanish. Every day will be Chanukah, and everyone will emanate chayn, while being exhilarated by the non-stop love of God.

THOUGH SOCIETIES RISE and fall because of definitions, people tend to ignore their importance. Imagine just how many relationships might not have ended or wrongly started had each side known the proper definition of love. Love is about a lot more than feeling good about someone else.

The English word doesn't tell the whole story. The word love comes from the Middle English word luf, which was derived from the Old English lufu. It is similar to the Old High German luba, and another Old English word, lēof, which means dear.[1]

---

[1] The English word "love" is based on classical Greek concepts of eros (passionate love); storge (familial love); philia (brotherly love, as friendship or affection); and agape (love of God for man and of man for God). Philautia is a variant meaning self-love.

The Hebrew word for love is ahavah.[2] However, when you look at the spelling of ahavah, Aleph-Heh-Bais-Heh, you notice that there is more to this word than its conventional meaning, which makes it more instructive. The root of the word is Heh-Bais, which means "give," because, as everyone is supposed to know, love is about giving, not receiving. The moment love is about what a person gets, it ceases to be love and instead becomes a business deal.

This may make it seem as if love is a one-way street, but it is not. On the contrary, a love relationship means that both parties want to love and be loved, which means that both sides are supposed to be giving. Each side has to be concerned only with its OWN giving, not that of the other person in the relationship.

This is crucial, which is why the yetzer hara fights against it. The yetzer hara would like you to believe that love is possible if you give only when you really have to, because it lives with the mistaken notion that giving means giving up and loss. It does not realize that true love is a function of the soul, and the soul is a function of divine light, which is unlimited. Soul love, by definition, is unlimited. Infatuation is not.

Aside from being godly, altruistic giving accom-

---

[2] Modern usage is similar to that of English, with meanings including to have affection, sexually or otherwise; love; like; befriend; to be intimate.

plishes something very profound, also indicated by the spelling of the Hebrew word. Each letter has its own numerical value, so Aleph-Heh-Bais-Heh together has a value: 1+5+2+5=13, the same as the word "echad," which means "one." It turns out that love, like da'as, is the power to unify.[3]

And unity is ESSENTIAL for love. Just as electricity needs a means to travel from its source to a receiver, love too needs a way to travel from one person to another. And just as an electrical charge weakens with distance and interference, love likewise loses its ability to connect if a person is spiritually distant and allows extraneous aspects of life to interfere with love.

Earlier we mentioned that it is the virtue of others that draws out our love for them. The love is an emotional pleasure that we feel when we see virtue in others. But that is another way of saying that love is that wonderfully positive feeling that we feel in our body when our soul connects to another soul and unifies with it.

The body wants to walk away from that and not hear it. It is used to physical pleasure as a method to keep life exciting because most bodies don't know much else. But as Kabbalah explains, what the body takes for granted is what makes physical pleasure so enjoyable—the spiritual element with which the body

---

[3] See Chapter 2.

is supposed to be imbued.

That's why it feels good to be part of a team. That is what makes shalom bayis so exhilarating. Yes, unity breeds synergy and therefore efficiency, and that too brings positive feelings. But the deeper pleasure is shared love, not as activity but as a state of being. It's pure bliss. We'll call it echadness.

Echadness is what makes cults so successful. Like idol worship, complete abandonment to group-think offers an illicit way to get a good thing. Idol worship seems to satisfy man's desire for a godly connection without the need for personal improvement. It's religion on man's terms, not God's.

Likewise, a cult fills the need of people to belong to a unit, to achieve oneness and unity without doing the work to make it happen. Instead, people abandon their wills and personalities to some central figure or cause, and they do what others around them are doing. It's like achieving shalom bayis by becoming a zombie. It may seem peaceful but it is no marriage.

Remember the story of Rebi Akiva who, while being tortured by the Romans, left this world saying echad from the Shema?[4] Remember how students questioned him, asking "Even here?" Perhaps Rebi Akiva wasn't only confirming the unity of God but the unity of his soul with God as well. Maybe through his

---

[4] Chapters 1 and 5.

supreme act of mesiras nefesh–self-sacrifice (literally giving of the soul), his soul joined with the reality of God as much as humanly possible.

This would explain on a deeper level the reason the Talmud concludes that Rebi was ready for eternal life. It doesn't just say he was going to the World-to-Come, as it does for others elsewhere. It uses the specific term Chaye Olamim–eternal life. All walls between Rebi Akiva and God came down that day, unifying his soul with God and freeing him to go straight to the World-to-Come, WITHOUT any time in Gehinom.

Simply put, God gives us a soul so that we can give it back to Him:

> The Rabbis taught, "And the spirit returns to God Who gave it" [Koheles 12:7]; give it to Him as He gave it to you; [just as He gave it to you] in purity, you too [should return it to God] in purity. There is a parable of a king of flesh and blood who distributed royal garments to his servants. The wise ones folded them and placed them in a box [to protect them, whereas] the foolish ones went and worked in them. After a period of time the king requested that his garments [be returned to him]. The wise ones returned them pressed, [as they were when they received them, and] the foolish ones returned them dirty. The king was happy to greet the wise ones and angry

to greet the foolish ones. (Shabbos 152b)

Receiving a soul is the easy part because it has nothing to do with us. Returning a soul is more difficult, and has EVERYTHING to do with us, especially since the Torah ruled out suicide. Since we're not allowed to just give back our life, we have to take care of it and develop it, being sure not to abuse our health. Thus we have a viable and valiant way to give our soul back to God…even while keeping it.

In fact, not only do you KEEP your soul with mesiras nefesh, you actually come to "own" it even more. You become more "echad" with it and, here's the funny part, more in love with YOURSELF, or more accurately, with your SELF. THIS is what makes people truly relaxed, confident in their manner of presenting themselves, or to use the modern-day idiom, "comfortable in their own skins."

We YEARN to live life like this—uninhibited, unaffected by what others think about who we are and what we do. We love it so much that some people actually cut themselves off from the judgmental world around them in order to try to be themselves, or go to the other extreme, doing whatever they want AS IF no one else were around them.

The rest of the world, and we're talking about billions of people over the ages, are in personal pain as they work hard to maintain personas that have been dictated by the world outside them. It gets to a point where even THEY start to believe the lie, and are stuck impersonating people they are not.

That is why crises, as dangerous as they can be, are also so refreshing. They literally tell the body, "Okay, step aside. We have no time for your shtick right now. We need to be as real as we can be as we try to solve the problem before us." The body has no choice in a crisis but to obey the order, other than to look completely out of place if it doesn't, similar to someone more worried about dirtying his clothes than stopping the bleeding of an injured person near him.

As we learn from Purim, da'as melts the layers. As we learn from Chanukah, mesiras nefesh and teshuvah cast them aside. Both accomplish the same thing, going more directly to the essence of our existence, our soul. So it's not only a matter of coming home, but actually a matter of finding our true self and then being it. There is no greater pleasure than making all our parts line up as they are meant to.

No greater pleasure because, as we said, when we're in touch with our soul, we're in touch with the ultimate love, of which the soul is a part. Not only that, but we gain access to another dimension of reality to which the soul belongs, the ETERNAL reality of the World-to-Come,[5] and when that pleasure makes it to

---

[5] See my book "Mindfulness, Torah, and Redemption."

the body, it is overwhelming in a good kind of way.

This also allows Shabbos to be such an uplifting experience for those who take full advantage of it. Shabbos is considered to be one-sixtieth of the World-to-Come,[6] making it a potential portal to the life of the seventh millennium, the first stage of eternal life.

But not for everyone. Divine light flows to those who can receive it, and that takes preparation. Showering and getting dressed especially for Shabbos helps, as do the fancy meals for the honor of Shabbos. But the main preparation a person must do to access the light of Shabbos and the World-to-Come is to act like a ben Olam HaBa, someone who deserves to go there.

That's what Torah and mitzvos principally accomplish. Yes, there is reward for doing them. But more than that, Torah and mitzvos help a person to peel back the layers of physicality that encase his soul, to expose it, to put him in touch with it so that he can simply be himself because, after all, echadness begins at home.

And when it does, people become natural givers. Selfishness is a function of the lack of sense of self, which forces people to define themselves by externalities. Then what they own becomes part of

---

[6] Brochos 53b.

them, making such things hard to give up and driving them to constantly strive to get more.

The soul is from infinite light. While quite the oxymoron—since infinity is indivisible—the soul is also quite miraculous. It's like having access to a spiritual internet, allowing you to stand in one place and have access to realities far beyond, as long as there is kli-tah–reception. If your computer or phone lacks the ability to go online, you won't reach past your loca-tion. Likewise a person who is not tuned into his soul won't relate to any reality beyond the one he is in. He won't have spiritual klitah.

Although we have one personal soul, that soul has FIVE parts,[7] like five rungs on a ladder between a person and God. They are the system that God uses to share His light with us, so that we can live and hopefully accomplish something meaningful with our life.

All five sections of soul must remain spiritually connected to one another for God's light to reach a person and keep him alive. The top level receives the light directly from God, and then filters it before pass-ing the remainder of the light to the next level, which then does the same thing before passing God's light to the next one. That is the way it works all the way

---

[7] Their Hebrew names are nefesh, ruach, neshamah, chayah, and yechidah. See my book "Reincarnation Clarified."

down to the bottom level in the body itself.

That's the automatic part. What is not automatic is how high up a person can access the light of his own soul. The more he does, the more life-energy he will access, and the more he will enhance his personal ability to spiritually accomplish. That determines how great he can become.

If you walk into a bank and request a large food platter, you will end up leaving the bank without even a small one, unless it is a food bank! You will need to go to a restaurant for something like that.

But if you go into a bank and request money, and you have some in your account, you will walk out with what you were looking for. You can even ask for a few thousand dollars and have your request fulfilled, so long as the money is in your account.

If, however, you ask for the $100,000 which is in your account, you will probably be required to come back later. The bank doesn't keep large sums of money on the premises, but rather needs to order them from reserve before delivery to you.

Why do you want extra money?

No one needs to ask that question. We know that the more money you have to spend, the more things you can purchase. The more things you can purchase, the greater your quality of life will be, and that's what life is all about, QUALITY OF LIFE, isn't it?

You wouldn't necessarily know it by the way

many people live their lives, even people with the ability to buy just about anything they want. They may be
high up on the financial scale, but quite low on the
soul scale. They may assume they are getting the best
of life when they are actually being distracted from it.
As the Talmud says, not too many people eat at two
tables—the physical one and the spiritual one—at the
same time.[8]

Quality of life is defined by a person's spiritual
fulfillment. Although by definition the spiritual potential of one person is not the same as that of another,
we're all equal in personal perfection, which is just that
—personal. The goal is to use the potential we have,
regardless of the potential someone else has.

Our soul, with all its parts, is the totality of our
personal potential. The more we access levels of our
soul, the more of our potential we access as well. And
just as increased materialism changes our outlook on
life and how we use it—not always for the better—increased soul-access does so even more, in the most
positive way possible.

Now comes the REALLY interesting part. Climb-
ing the soul ladder not only increases spiritual potential, greatness, and fulfillment. It also increases our access to other dimensions of reality, specifically to the
World-to-Come. WE may be stuck in the present, but

---

[8] Brochos 5b.

our higher levels of soul are not.

The fabric of reality changes and becomes more spiritual as our consciousness ascends from level to level, and time also changes for us. It's quite simple. The closer we are to God, the more we approach the eternal. The farther we move from God, the more physical our existence becomes, and the more time-bound we are.

Therefore, as we access higher levels of soul, we access more eternal realities. Eventually we can begin to access the reality of the World-to-Come, which begins on the third lowest level of soul, neshamah. It is also the level from which teshuvah emanates, meaning that when we do teshuvah, we access this level of light as well, the one that corresponds to the holiday of Yom Kippur.

As to be expected from such high levels of light, echadness is the result. Levels of soul unify, and we have a sense of being more whole and more spiritual. We will still walk the same earth we have always walked, but our consciousness will be leagues above what it once was, and more timeless.

In fact this level corresponds to something Kabbalah calls heichal ahavah, literally hall of love. It is the level that few ever reach during their lifetimes, but those who do know love of God beyond any other love experienced. To be one with our soul is to be one with God. There is no greater love than this.

Prayer of Love

THE TALMUD DESCRIBES prayer as "something that stands at the heights of the world, but people disgrace it."[1] Apparently this is not something unique to our generation, so far away from the period of prophecy. Even in Second Temple times, tefillah—prayer was under-appreciated.

The chassidei rishonim,[2] on the other hand, would take a full hour to prepare for prayer, another hour to pray, and one hour to leave it.[3] Not only did they not disgrace prayer, they made it the priority of their day, and they were VERY busy people.

To outsiders, people who don't really know what

---

[1] Brochos 6b.

[2] Early pious ones.

[3] Brochos 32b.

prayer is about, evidenced by the way they pray, these pious people just seemed, well, pious. Outsiders assumed it wasn't that these pious prayers knew something special about prayer, gaining something so fantastic from it that they couldn't wait to pray again. It was more that they made a bigger deal out of prayer than most, for some strange personal reasons.

That's the problem with spiritual experiences. It's hard to share them with someone who hasn't had them yet. Because they are so personal, others who have yet to experience such internal events will not even know they exist, let alone appreciate them. But it doesn't hurt to talk about them anyhow.

The Mishkan–Tabernacle provides a good analogy. It was comprised of four areas: (1) the Holy of Holies where the Holy Ark was located; (2) the Sanctuary in which the Menorah, showbread table, and golden altar were placed; (3) the Courtyard where the large altar was situated; and (4) the world beyond its curtained enclosure, where everyday life continued.

From outside the curtain it was impossible to see what was going on inside. Observing was possible only if people entered the Courtyard within the curtains, and that could happen only if they first properly purified themselves. Otherwise they had to remain outside and at most use their limited imaginations.

People who entered the Courtyard could watch the daily service of sacrifices performed by the kohanim, but they could not see into the Sanctuary beyond the Courtyard. Nor could they enter it, because only kohanim could enter that part of the Mishkan proper. Even the undefiled non-kohanim could only guess at what went on inside the sanctuary in connection with the kindling of the Menorah, the removal and placing of the showbread, and the golden-altar service.

But that was as far as the kohanim could go, even the Kohen Gadol—except for once a year on Yom Kippur. That was the one time of year that the Kohen Gadol was supposed to enter the Holy of Holies as part of the Yom Kippur service. Everyone else had only their imaginations to try to appreciate what it was like to be in such close proximity to God while in this world.

The tefillah experience works in a similar way. There are people who treat prayer to God like a job which they would prefer not to do, but have to do anyway because it is an obligation. If they weren't afraid of the consequences for not praying, they wouldn't take the time to do it, which they minimize anyhow. Their hearts just aren't in it, so why should God's be? Thus they have NO idea what a real tefillah-experience actually is.

There are people who at least go beyond the initial curtain into the courtyard of prayer. They take tefillah seriously enough to treat it as more than just a daily obligation. They make a point of understanding the words, but still do not believe enough in prayer's impact on life to invest much of themselves in it.

Then there are the people who do realize the potential of prayer to access the presence of God. They know that the formalized words are simply a means to the end, the body of prayer into which they have to breathe their souls to give it life. Fueled by a love of God, they put their hearts into their tefillah, turning prayer into an opportunity, rather than an un-avoidable obligation.

That in itself is a major accomplishment, and a pretty rare one today. And yet it is not the ultimate level, just as the Sanctuary was not the highest level of holiness in the Mishkan. There was still the Kodesh Kodashim, the Holy of Holies, and the same is true of tefillah, the level of prayer of the chassidei rishonim.

On this level people do not merely pray TO God. They CONNECT to God, feeling a very real at-tachment and also a tremendous amount of love FROM God. People who have reached this level speak about a desire not to return to the everyday world, which seems incredibly mundane and petty after such a phenomenal, godly experience. Parting is very difficult for them after they were enwrapped in such a close experience with the Creator.

In truth the morning prayer experience is ar-ranged to promote such an ascension through prayer, and the afternoon and evening services as well, although less so. The morning service has four levels built into the order, and if people understand how they are meant to progress, their tefillah can become an otherworldly experience every day.

It starts with the morning blessings and sacrifices found in all siddurim. People are just starting their day, and many feel the most like bodies then—more sluggish and tired, not spiritually inspired—than they will during the rest of the day. With the proper focus and intention, they will be elevated to the next level, Pesukei d'Zimra, the Introductory Psalms.

The concepts are loftier in Pesukei d'Zimra, consisting of selections from Tehillim by Dovid HaMelech, who perhaps knew the love of God best of all. They are the words of a man who longed to be as attached to God as is humanly possible. If we pay attention to what he said, how he instructed us, then by the end of Pesukei d'Zimra we should find ourselves ready to soar with the angels who LIVE to praise God.

At least that is where we are supposed to be by the time we enter the level of Birchas Krias Shema, the section of the Shema and its blessings. Yes, it is more likely that at the speed of most minyanim and the lack of focus of many people, they will race through this section just like those before it. But it is also possible for people in pursuit of the love of God to use this section to reach high levels of spiritual consciousness.

There's not much time to do it, though. The average minyan these days takes about two to three minutes to go from Borchu to Ga'al Yisroel and Shemoneh Esrai, the climax of the prayer service. By that time, people have to be ready to completely detach themselves from all worldly matters and be as much with God as possible.

Unfortunately, by the time many step into Shemoneh Esrai, they are like people who just happened to stumble into the king's palace without really knowing where they actually are. If they knew, even those unlearned would act differently during tefillah, but especially at this time. They would pray as if their lives depended on it, which they do.

The problem is that at this late stage of history we don't get a clear view—if any at all—of the impact mitzvos have on our life and the world in general. It's as if they once did, but today we just continue on with tradition to preserve the Torah way of life until it can become real for us again. There's only so much people can invest in something strenuous when it seems to be futile.

This is especially true of tefillah. If people knew that when they pray, God not only listens and takes note, but He actually answers prayers which are sincere, they would pray accordingly. "If He does answer," many people think, "then it's a secret to me!"

Some people, however, do not need to see signs of God's involvement in prayer to know that He is indeed involved, regardless of what they get back in return. They make the effort anyway, work hard to focus deeply, and are amazed at what happens when they turn to God with that kind of approach. They receive love from God.

Perhaps what some forget, or never realized, is that the entire process begins with them:

> One who comes to purify himself, they help him. (Yoma 38b)

This means that the level of connection to God we are talking about is possible only when people take steps to achieve it. When God sees that, then He moves toward them. As it says:

> The sacrifices of God are a broken spirit. (Tehillim 51:17)

Humility is crucial to the process. Awe is absolutely essential. That is what transforms people from being self-focused to being God-centered. People act differently in front of a CEO who is worth a few million dollars than they do in the presence of a CEO who is worth a few billion dollars. Millions of dollars represent success. Billions of dollars represent incredible success and lot of power. That awes people.

And yet billions of dollars aren't even comparable to a few cents when contrasted with the awesomeness of God. It's just that multi-billionaires make the Forbes 500 and God doesn't. The former get a lot of press and are spotted from time to time by those who worship them, but God isn't. And for many people, out of sight is out of mind.

That's where tefillah can and should come in. It takes work and time, but tefillah is the means to put God back into the minds of people. When that happens, God stops being out of sight. God is never actually visible to anyone, not even to a prophet like Moshe Rabbeinu. But there are different types of seeing, and this one is a lot more powerful than the one with the eyes.

The prophet, speaking about the Messianic Era, said:

> God will be King over the entire land. And on that day, God will be One, and His Name, One. (Zechariah 14:9)

Of course He will be then. With the yetzer hara out of the way, the veil comes down and EVERYONE will see God for himself. With all spiritual interpositions out of the way, connection to God will be automatic and continuous. We won't need formalized tefillah at that time to bridge the gap between us and the Creator. WE ourself will be the bridge, and the love between God and His central creation will flow both ways at maximum capacity.

Dovid HaMelech also wrote:

> As for me, may my prayer to You, O God, be at an acceptable time. (Tehillim 69:14)

That is the traditional way to read the verse. But the Hebrew could also be read as "and I am my prayer…" because everyone should be so at one with his prayer and true to himself that it is revealed in his appearance and actions. Prayer is called avodas halev, the service of the heart. The heart is what drives a person, and wherever the heart goes, the person will surely follow.

On this side of history we need to actually pray. It focuses us, inspires us, and brings our emotions to the forefront when it is done correctly, sincerely. But that's because we have to fight against the yetzer hara which does everything it possibly can to intercede between us and God.

Once the yetzer hara is gone, people will naturally yearn for God, and bask in the light and love of God. That is when people will be their own prayers, making their connections profound and love-filled.

AND THEN THERE is the Land of Love, Eretz Yisroel. It was given to Avraham Avinu and his descendants as a gift of love from God. Called the Palace of the King, the Jewish people were invited to move right in to live with the King, God Himself.

In an atlas of the world, Israel is but one VERY small portion of land, albeit strategically located. Although it is not the most fertile land, it can be quite mountainous and has a fair bit of desert. It has some great beaches and fantastic views, but other than that, the land does not seem all that PHYSICALLY prestigious. If God hadn't made such a big deal about it, would anyone else have?

No. But then again, isn't what GOD thinks about something the WHOLE point? What makes anything at all important or unimportant in this world is what its Maker says about it. If God likes something, we should love it. If He doesn't, neither should we.

This is what God Himself said about Eretz Yisroel:

> The land you are about to possess is not like Egypt from where you came and in which, if you sowed seeds, you had to bring water to them as you would for a garden of green herbs. The land you are about to possess has mountains and deep valleys, and is watered by rain from the sky —a land which God, your God, cares for, and God, your God, pays attention to continuously the entire year. (Devarim 11:11-12)

To be clear, God takes care of the ENTIRE world. What the verses mean is what the Talmud explains:

> God personally waters Eretz Yisroel. The rest of the nations receive their sustenance through a messenger. (Ta'anis 10a)

And not just any messenger, but a spiritually IM-PURE one, an angel from the side of impurity. All angels appointed over the nations of the world to look out for their interests in heaven come from the side of impurity, the Overseer of Eretz Yisroel being the exception. He's not only from the side of purity, He is the essence of it.

If a person truly understands life, the conversation should end here. Though these are but two of countless statements about the spiritual benefit of living in Eretz Yisroel, they basically sum it up. I mean, what other land can promise you the World-to-Come,[1] or that just breathing its air will make you wise?[2] Wisdom is essential for a meaningful life, and a meaningful life is necessary for going to the World-to-Come.

To appreciate what living in Eretz Yisroel should mean to a Jew, there is this:

So said God, "Where is your mother's bill of divorce, that I sent her away?" (Yeshaya 50:1)

This was said to the nation as it entered Bavel, its first exile after coming into Eretz Yisroel. The people wondered if they were now free to leave Torah behind and adopt the values of their host society, God told them otherwise: "We are still married. We are not divorced. You rebelled, so I temporarily sent you away. Make amends and you will come back

---

[1] Kesuvos 111a; Pesachim 113a. See my book on the topic, "Talking About Eretz Yisroel" for more details.

[2] Bava Basra 158b.

home."[3]

Married? To God? Since when?

Since Mt. Sinai. God was the groom, the Jewish people were considered to be His bride, and the Torah was the marriage document, never to be rescinded. When the spies rejected Eretz Yisroel, it was similar to a bride telling her husband, "Let's live in separate houses." It doesn't make for very good shalom bayis, no matter how loyal the spouses remain to each other and honor the terms of the kesuvah.

Thus the Torah says:

I am God, your God, Who took you out of the land of Egypt to give you the land of Canaan, to be God to you. (Vayikra 25:38)

This is not a limitation of God. This is a choice of God. He's not saying here that He CAN'T be our God in the Diaspora. He's saying that He WON'T be our God there, because God can do anything He wants, wherever He wants, any time He wants. He is saying, "If you want me to be your PERSONAL God, then you have to come to Eretz Yisroel."

If this weren't the case, would there be a difference between exile and redemption? Let's face it,

---

[3] Malbim.

some people prefer other lands to Eretz Yisroel. They prefer the West over the Middle East. You don't move to Eretz Yisroel for the view, because there are far better ones elsewhere. You don't move to Eretz Yisroel for the sun, because there are other warm places. And until recently you did not move to Israel for security reasons.

Israel is not famous for its geographical advantages. It is special for its spiritual advantage, because it is THE home of God's Presence in this world. It is not possible to build a Temple to God anywhere else in the world but Eretz Yisroel, and in no city other than in Jerusalem. He's had HIS embassy in Jerusalem ever since Shlomo HaMelech built the first version of it.

Yes, it is possible to build a huge yeshivah just about anywhere in the world. Yes, it is possible to fill yeshivos with God-fearing, Torah-loving Jews who can learn just as well, if not better, than their counterparts in Eretz Yisroel. But this still cannot make up for learning Torah in the Land of God, which is why God punished us with exile in the first place. The fact that people have found a way to enjoy their punishment is to their detriment, not God's.

The spies made that catastrophic mistake. They had no intention of abandoning God or Torah, which is why they thought that abandoning Eretz Yisroel would not cost them. If it had occurred to them that from God's perspective, rejecting the Land lessened the quality of their relationship to God and Torah, would they have done it? That would have been suicide, no?

There is a reason the rabbis living in the Diaspora wrote:

> Three good gifts were given to the Jewish people, and each of them is acquired through suffering: Torah, Eretz Yisroel, and the World-to-Come. (Brochos 5a)

Though they had built the biggest and most prosperous yeshivos in history to date, the rabbis of Bavel wanted it to be clear that they never felt these could be replacements for living in Eretz HaKodesh, the Holy Land. They were in Bavel by divine decree, and every day they yearned to return to the land of their fathers, the land of THE Father.

And they worded their statement as they did to emphasize a second point. Torah is the lifeline of the Jewish people in any generation, whether we have the merit to live on the land, or not. But one thing is clear: The path to the World-to-Come may start with Torah, but it passes through Eretz Yisroel, where Torah is best learned and mitzvos are best performed.

Why? If a person is learning just as well in the Diaspora as he would in Eretz Yisroel, why move? If a person is living a successful life as a Torah Jew in chutz l'aretz, perhaps able to perform mitzvos more fully outside the land than in the land, why change that? What does Eretz Yisroel give a Jew that the Diaspora just can't match?

Love of God, both from the person to God and from God to the person. If the Diaspora is a place where God reduces His visibility in the life of Jews, it means that they will have greater difficulty connecting the events of their lives with Divine Providence. It will be harder to feel as emotionally moved by the good from God as they might feel intellectually and, as a result, even the intellectual connection will fade over time.

Eretz Yisroel is the land of Hashgochah Pratis, Divine Providence. It is the land of bitachon, trust in God. Even if the Shechinah–Divine Presence goes into exile with the Jewish people, it is mostly to protect them from the spiritual dangers of living in exile. It is not to create a duplicate reality of Eretz Yisroel.

On his way to Lavan's house Ya'akov Avinu even tried to convince God to deal with him as if he were still in Eretz Yisroel, but he was only partially successful. It took "wild horses" to drag him from his beloved land, which is more than can be said for many others since. And though God gave him first-class protection, exile still remained exile for him. He couldn't wait to get back home and returned at the first opportunity he had.

True, Ya'akov was a prophet who spoke with God. True, he also had known Eretz Yisroel on a level that we can't. And true, his Diaspora was not nearly as Jew-friendly as ours has been for the last 70 years or so. But it is untrue that we lack the capacity to make up for all this, at least on some level.

That is where the Ramban's explanation can come in. He asks a simple question based on the following verses, but comes to a wonderfully insightful and instructive conclusion that all Jews, especially during times of exile, should take to heart.

The first verse is part of Moshe Rabbeinu's instructions to the spies. He's advising them how to approach their precarious mission, and adds:

See—urisem the land—what it is. (Bamidbar 13: 18)

Then later, at the end of the parshah after the entire disastrous episode of the spies and with respect to the mitzvah of tzitzis, the Torah says:

"It shall be tzitzis for you, and you shall see—urisem it [techeles] and remember all the mitzvos and do them." (Bamidbar 15:39)

Why, the Ramban asks, is the word, urisem—see

used in both contexts?[4] In most books, the double usage might not mean anything. But in the Torah, the same word used in two different locations usually connects them on some conceptual level and has to mean something significant.

The Ramban begins answering the question by quoting the following:

> Rebi Meir used to say: What is unique about techeles with respect to all other colors? The sea is blue, which is like the sky, which is like the Throne of Glory, as it says, "And under His feet was the likeness of sapphire, brickwork, and it was like the essence of heaven in purity" [Shemos 24:10], and it says, "The appearance of sapphire stone in the likeness of a throne" [Yechezkel 1:26]. (Menachos 43b)

The single techeles thread on each corner of tzitzis is the Torah's solution to "spying after one's eyes." A Jew is supposed to be able to look at a single blue thread with his physical eyes and imagine the Throne of Glory in his mind's eye. The physical world we see is just a veil for the invisible reality of God that permeates every aspect of Creation and imbues it with holiness.

---

4 Ramban, Bamidbar 13:1.

This capacity to look past the misleading physical reality and see—with the help of the imagination—the true spiritual reality is what Moshe Rabbeinu hinted about to the spies. If they had not been blinded by all the physical issues they came back and reported on, they would have seen the intrinsic kedushah in every rock, tree, and river instead. Like Yehoshua and Caleiv, the other 10 spies would have been eager to enter and settle Eretz Yisroel, rather than reject it.

Even more, the 10 spies would have felt the love of God rather than fear of the land's inhabitants. But as everyone knows, the rejecter of love also repels the sender of that love. The greater the love, the more those who reject it run in the opposite direction.

Here is a more recent story to this effect.

A young man travelled to Israel to explore the land. He was not religious and had no intention of changing that. He came for the fun and cheap travel before continuing on with a planned cross-Europe trip.

From the moment he got off the plane, however, he felt uneasy. There was something about being in Israel that made him uncomfortable, which he chalked up to being in a Middle-Eastern country. He assumed that once he acclimatized somewhat, he would feel better.

It didn't happen. Not only did he not feel more

at home in Israel, but he found that the uncomfortable feeling intensified when he got to Jerusalem. It
didn't make any difference what he did, what he ate,
or how much fun he had. He just felt like running
away.

So he did. He cut his trip short and headed for
Greece instead. As soon as the plane was in the air,
he felt more relaxed again…though he did have an
eerie feeling that he would be back.

He travelled through Europe as planned and
then headed home a month later. Europe had been
distracting, but something about the Israeli part of the
trip stayed with him, even haunting him to some degree.

To make a long story shorter, after getting back
home, the young man began to attend classes on
Torah Judaism purely by hashgochah pratis.[5] But one
class led to another and then another, and eventually
a Shabbos and another Shabbos. About nine months
later, he realized that he had been mistaken about
Torah, had learned enough to begin to embrace it,
and started his path to teshuvah.

At one point he felt that he could not learn or
grow fast enough where he was living. That was be-

---

[5] Divine providence, a series of unlikely events, in this case
brought about for someone who thought he had no interest
whatsoever in Torah Judaism—or any Judaism for that matter.

fore learning centers geared to his pace of spiritual growth had been opened, so he decided to go to a yeshivah in Eretz Yisroel.

This time, touching down on Israeli soil was a whole different experience. Not only did he not feel uncomfortable, he actually felt warmly embraced. He no longer felt like running away from Eretz Yisroel, but rather like running toward it.

It didn't take long for him to figure out the reason for the difference. The previous year he hadn't wanted God's love. On the contrary, it made him feel uneasy because it meant something very religious to him, and he had rejected things like that since he quit participating in anything even remotely Jewish.

In the course of a year that had changed. He discovered his misconceptions about life and Torah, and did a complete about-face, choosing to learn it instead and live by its mitzvos. All of a sudden, love of God was not something to be avoided but pursued to the greatest extent until his last breath. It now felt WONDERFUL to get such a big dose of love just by showing up at the King's Palace.

He came to Eretz Yisroel for the love of God.

For the love of God, he found it.

THE FOLLOWING TITLES are all the books written over the years. Some books may no longer be in print, but many are still available in either PDF or Kindle formats. Visit the Thirtysix.org OnLine Bookstore, or Amazon for more information, or to order online.

The Unbroken Chain of Jewish Tradition, 1985
The Eternal Link, 1990
If Only I Were Wealthy, 1992
If Only I Understood Why, 1993
If Only I Could See the Forest, 1993
If Only I Could Stay, 1993
If Only Great Was Greater, 1993
The Y Factor, 1994
Life's A Thrill, 1994

No Atheists in a Foxhole, 1994
Changes that Last Forever, 1994
The Making of a Great Jewish Leader, 1994
Bereishis: A Beginning With No End, 1994
The Wonderful World of Thirtysix, 1995
Redemption to Redemption, 1997
The Big Picture, 1998
Perceptions, 1998
Not Just Another Scenario, 2001
At The Threshold, 2001
Anticipating Redemption, 2002
Sha'ar HaGilgulim, 2002
Hadran (Hebrew), 2004
Talking About The End of Days, 2005
Talking About Eretz Yisroel, 2005
The Physics of Kabbalah, 2006
Be Positive, 2007
Geulah b'Rachamim, 2007
God.calm, 2007
Just Passing Through, 2007
On The Same Page, 2007
The Equation of Life, 2007
No Such Victim, 2009
Survival in 10 Easy Steps, 2009
Not Just Another Scenario 2, 2011
All In Your Mind, 2011
The Light of Thirtysix, 2011
The Last Exile, 2011

Drowning in Pshat, 2012
Drown No More, 2012
Shas Man, 2013
The Mystery of Jewish History, 2013
Survival Guide For the End-of-Days, 2013
Deeper Perceptions, 2013
Chanukah Lite, 2015
The Hitchhiker's Guide to Armageddon, 2016
Purim Lite, 2016
Pesach Lite, 2016
The Torah Empowerment Seminar, 2016
Siman Tov (Hebrew), 2016
The Fabric of Reality, 2016
Addendum, 2016
Fundamentals of Reincarnation, 2017
Reincarnation Clarified, 2016
All About Energy, 2017
What Goes Around, 2017
The God Experience, 2017
What in Heaven, 2017
The God Experience, Part 2, 2017
The God Experience, Part 3, 2017
It's About Time, 2017
Need to Know, 2017
Perceptions, Volume 2, 2017
Once Revealed, Twice Concealed, 2017
The Art of Chayn, 2017
A Matter of Laugh or Death, 2018

Geulah b'Rachamim Program, V. 1, 2018
Geulah b'Rachamim Program, V. 2, 2018
Geulah b'Rachamim Program, V. 3, 2018
Point of Acceptance, 2018
See Ya, 2018
In Discussion: Bereishis, 2018
Reincarnation Again, 2018
A Separate Matter, 2018
In Discussion: Shemos, 2019
A Search for Self, 2019
A Search for Trust, 2019
In Discussion: Bamidbar, 2019
How It Might Play Out, 2019
In Discussion: Vayikra, 2019
Where Are My Emotions Now, 2019
In Discussion: Devarim, 2019
The Early Years, 2019
Oh, So Blind, 2019
Not So Bad? 2019
Sha'ar HaPesukim: Shemos, 2019
The Fix, 2020
Sha'ar HaPesukim: Bereishis, 2020
Preparing For Redemption, 2020
Mindfulness, Torah & Redemption, 2020
Moment of Moments, 2020
For the Love of God, 2020

For more information: pinchasw@thirtysix.org,

thirtysix.org

www.ingramcontent.com/pod-product-compliance
Lightning Source LLC
Chambersburg PA
CBHW072007170726
47999CB00013B/514